T0114980

REVELATION
OF THE
BIBLE
THE BOOK OF GENESIS

MOSHE MAZIN

REVELATION OF THE BIBLE
THE BOOK OF GENESIS

iUniverse books may be ordered through booksellers or by contacting:
iUniverse
1663 Liberty Drive
Bloomington, IN 47403
www.iuniverse.com
1-800-Authors (1-800-288-4677)

ISBN: 978-1-4502-8559-9 (sc)
ISBN: 978-1-4502-8558-2 (hc)
ISBN: 978-1-4502-8560-5 (e)

Library of Congress Control Number: 2011901687

Print information available on the last page.

iUniverse rev. date: 08/05/2016

This book is dedicated to my mother, Sarah HaLevi.

Your vision has come true.

Contents

Preface

This book contains my views and understanding of the book of Genesis. I do not claim to be a scholar in the field of theology or an accomplished researcher in the field of biblical studies. However, I do have original insights that provide explanations for the stories and writings of the Bible. These insights differ greatly from published material by various scholars throughout history.

I have written this book because of my need to know the truth, especially when it concerns my ancestors. There are countless explanations, commentaries, and theories about the Bible, but none of them provide a complete explanation for its stories. Even the well-known and highly regarded kabbalistic book of the Jewish Zohar attributed to Rabbi Simon Ben Yochi, who lived at the end of the first century AC (After Christ) does not deal directly with various passages in the Bible with unbiased perception. (This will become clear to readers when they read the various outcomes in the book of Genesis.)

Other well-known rabbis and scholars of Jewish and non-Jewish origin (Onkelos, 120–135 AC, nephew to the emperor Titus or Hadrian who converted to Judaism; Rabbi Shlomo Yitzhaki, or Rashi, of France, 1040–1105 AC; and Rabbi Moses Maimonides, or Rambam 1135–1204 AC) have commented on these and other events in much the same manner.

In reading the book of Genesis, readers should clear their minds of any previously established beliefs or notions. This is necessary if one is to understand the subtleties of the wording and the meaning behind the words in Genesis.

The book follows the biblical text of the book of Genesis. However, when it comes to the act of creation and the emergence of the ten sefirot, which are the ten dimensions of the universe, it expands on this subject to beyond what is written in Genesis.

I have followed the Hebrew text of Genesis and in some cases paraphrased the specific content of a sentence. The reason for not including any English translation of the Hebrew text is that there are many such translations and they vary in their interpretations. Therefore, choosing a specific version may not be sufficiently accurate for the purpose of detailed insights.

The reader should choose a version of the English translation, and if a certain quote or statement is not found in that version, he or she may choose to search other versions, including the Hebrew text, to ensure the accuracy of the quotes or statements.

I have examined the writings of the four rabbis and scholars of the Bible mentioned above as sources of commentary on the Bible. In many cases, there is agreement between my writings and those of the above-mentioned scholars, and in other cases there is no agreement on the actual events that transpired in Genesis. In this book, I provide interpretations and point out secrets that have been hidden from the public at large for many generations.

To explain creation, I provide both scientific and biblical accounts. The scientific account keeps the basic science to an outline of the various concepts, such as the big bang theory, string theory, the Heisenberg principle of uncertainty regarding quantum theory, and so on, whereas the biblical account is more detailed. The reason for the short outline of the scientific theories is that most people will not understand the detailed scientific formulas of general relativity and those of the more recent string theory, or quantum theory and the central theme of the

Heisenberg principle of uncertainty. In contrast, the biblical creation dives into more details that can be understood by more people.

After these two concepts, the various events of Genesis are presented.

The maps and photos and the outline of the big bang and string theories in this book were taken from wikipedia.org and Bibleatlas.org.

The intention of using these short explanations and maps is to provide a framework for readers so that they understand the geographical terrain at that time.

I have also provided materials in support of the various ideas from websites, such as www.wikipedia.org, www.bibleatlas.org, www. occult-advances.org, www.wikiquate.org, www.bibleplaces.com, www. columbiauniversity.edu, www.fotosearch.com, www.iem-inc.com, www.asianenergy.blogspot.com, www.scribd.com, and others that are shown in the body of the text. I want to thank the Reverend Patricia Bertucci and Dr. Yitzhak Bakal for their encouragement and support.

Chapter 1 Creation of Something from Nothingness

Genesis 1 and 2

To understand creation in the book of Genesis, one needs to understand the meanings of the concept of nothingness. The reason for this is simple; the passage tells us that God has created something from nothing. This simple statement implies that nothing existed before God began creating.

The question, therefore, is, what is nothingness?

One could only use an analogy to grasp the concept of nothingness. This is because of the fact that it is impossible to define nothingness in simple terms. One can't define nothingness in terms of its opposite by saying that there is nothing there, or by saying that it is empty space, or by saying it is void of anything. Each of these words defines something but not nothing. It is similar to the concept of zero in mathematics, which parallels the concept of nothingness but is not the same. A discussion of the history of zero and the struggle that humanity had in defining it is given by Professor Robert Kaplan, author of *The Nothing That Is: A Natural History of Zero* and former professor of mathematics at Harvard University. Here is one paragraph of his article published in *Scientific American,* January 16, 2007:

"The mathematical zero and the philosophical notion of nothingness are related but are not the same. Nothingness plays a central role very early on in Indian thought (there it is called *sunya*), and we find speculation in virtually all cosmological myths about what must have preceded the world's creation. So it is written in the Bible's book of Genesis (1:2): 'And the earth was without form, and void.'"

Professor Kaplan sums it up well, but we still do not know what nothingness is. (The reader is encouraged to read Kaplan's article and book for better insight.)

It is clear that none of these definitions or explanations defines accurately the concept of nothingness. Therefore, we are forced to use an analogy to explain it.

Consider the following scenario: What if planet Earth was made only of water and a person was sitting in the center of the planet? Now then, when that person looks around, what does he see other than his own body?

The answer is obviously nothing.

Why is that so?

It is because the mind cannot form any geometric single point or line or three-dimensional structure of any kind within the body of water. It is clear that the reason for this phenomenon is that there is uniformity within the water. Therefore, we can say that nothingness is literally equal to absolute uniformity. This is only one half of the analogy. The other half that can further explain nothingness is discussed below.

To understand the other half of the analogy, consider the entire universe and fill it, in your imagination, with equal squares. Then erase the outline of those squares. What do you have? If one considers this exercise carefully, it becomes clear that once you erase all the outlines of the squares, all that remains is the universe itself. This, however, leads us to another concept, and that is the concept of ONE.

Now we have two concepts that we were not familiar with before: the concept of nothingness and the concept of one.

Why are these concepts important? The following sections attempt to clarify the answers both from the scientific and biblical viewpoints in regard to nothingness as an existence before creation and the concept of one relating to the entire creation itself.

Chapter 2   Scientific Account of Creation

The scientific and biblical accounts of creation are one and the same; however, they are viewed from two distinct points of reference. The scientific account is a bottom-up account of creation, whereas the biblical account is a top-down account. To understand this statement, consider the following two scenarios of a top-down account (biblical) and a bottom-up account (scientific) below. Note that the bottom-up view of creation that science offers has within it two views, that of the deterministic universe in accordance with Einstein's famous statement, "God does not play dice with the universe" and that of the quantum theory with its principle supposition, the Heisenberg principle of uncertainty, which is covered in the following sections. Please note that both of these views are correct. However, they must be viewed from their point of reference, top down versus bottom up. Einstein's statement was in regard to the top-down view of the universe.

2.1   What ignited the big bang?

It is well known that a spark of unknown origin ignited the big bang and brought existence and expansion to the universe. [1, 2, 3] We do not know how this spark came to be or what its origin was, but we do know that the result was a massive explosion that we call the big bang. The big bang caused the creation of matter and its expansion [4, 5] and in turn the formation of galaxies, various planets, and other heavenly bodies. We do not know what existed before the big bang. However, we do know that galaxies are moving away from each other, and that all combination of matter will deteriorate at the end of time to a frozen state or, if you wish, nothingness.[6] At this end-of-time state, we can say that no energy exists. Therefore, one can think of this state or end-of-existence state as a universe of nothingness, lacking any energy, therefore being in total darkness.

2.2 Very short review of the big bang theory

(start of article from Wikipedia)

Theory

The theoretical scientific exploration of the ultimate fate of the universe became possible with Albert Einstein's 1916 theory of general relativity. General relativity can be employed to describe the universe on the largest possible scale. There are many possible solutions to the equations of general relativity, and each solution implies a possible ultimate fate of the universe. Alexander Friedman proposed a number of such solutions in 1922 as did Georges Lemaître in 1927. In some of these the universe has been expanding from an initial singularity; this is, essentially, the Big Bang.

Observation

In 1931, Edwin Hubble published his conclusion, based on his observations of Cepheid variable stars in distant galaxies that the universe was expanding. From then on, the *beginning* of the universe and its possible *end* have been the subjects of serious scientific investigation.

Big Bang and Steady state theories

In 1927, Georges Lemaître set out a theory that has since come to be called the Big Bang theory of the origin of the universe. In 1948, Fred Hoyle set out his opposing steady state theory in which the universe continually expanded but remained statistically unchanged as new matter is constantly created. These two theories were active contenders until the 1965 discovery, by Arno Penzias and Robert Wilson, of the cosmic microwave background radiation, a fact that is a straightforward prediction of the Big Bang theory, and one that the original Steady State theory could not account for. As a result The Big Bang theory immediately became the most widely held view of the origin of the universe.

Cosmological constant

When Einstein formulated <u>general relativity</u>, he and his contemporaries believed in a static universe. When Einstein found that his equations could easily be solved in such a way as to allow the universe to be expanding now, and to contract in the far future, he added to those equations what he called a cosmological constant, essentially a constant energy density unaffected by any expansion or contraction, whose role was to offset the effect of gravity on the universe as a whole in such a way that the universe would remain static. After Hubble announced his conclusion that the universe was expanding, Einstein wrote that his cosmological constant was "the greatest blunder of my life." (George Gamow, *My World Line*, 1970).

Density parameter

An important parameter in fate of the universe theory is the Density parameter, Omega (Ω), defined as the average matter density of the universe divided by a critical value of that density. This selects one of three possible <u>geometries</u> depending on whether Ω is equal to, less than, or greater than 1. These are called, respectively, the flat, open and closed universes. These three adjectives refer to the overall geometry of the universe, and not to the local curving of space time caused by smaller clumps of mass (for example, galaxies and stars). If the primary content of the universe is inert matter, as in the <u>dust models</u> popular for much of the 20th century, there is a particular fate corresponding to each geometry. Hence cosmologists aimed to determine the fate of the universe by measuring Ω, or equivalently the rate at which the expansion was decelerating.

Repulsive force

Starting in 1998, observations of supernovae in distant galaxies have been interpreted as consistent with a universe whose expansion is accelerating. Subsequent cosmological theorizing has been designed so as to allow for this possible acceleration, nearly always by involving dark energy, which in its simplest form is just a positive cosmological constant. In general dark energy is a catch-all term for any hypothesized field with negative pressure, usually with a density that changes as the universe expands.

Role of the shape of the universe

See also: Shape of the universe

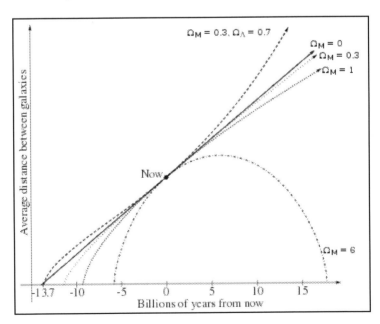

The ultimate fate of an expanding universe depends on the matter density Ω_M and the dark energy density Ω_Λ.

The current scientific consensus of most cosmologists is that the ultimate fate of the universe depends on its overall shape, how much dark energy it contains, and on the equation of state which determines how the dark energy density responds to the expansion of the universe. Recent observations have shown that, from 7.5 billion years after the Big Bang onwards, the expansion rate of the universe has actually been increasing, concurrent with the Open Universe theory.

Closed universe

If $\Omega > 1$, then the geometry of space is closed like the surface of a sphere. The sum of the angles of a triangle exceeds 180 degrees and there are no parallel lines; all lines eventually meet. The geometry of the universe is, at least on a very large scale, elliptic.

In a closed universe lacking the repulsive effect of dark energy, gravity eventually stops the expansion of the universe, after which it starts to contract until all matter in the universe collapses to a point, a final singularity termed the "Big Crunch," by analogy with Big Bang. However, if the universe has a large amount of dark energy (as suggested by recent findings) then the expansion of the universe can continue forever—even if $\Omega > 1$.

Open universe

If $\Omega < 1$, the geometry of space is open, i.e., negatively curved like the surface of a saddle. The angles of a triangle sum to less than 180 degrees, and lines that do not meet are never equidistant; they have a point of least distance and otherwise grow apart. The geometry of such a universe is hyperbolic.

Even without dark energy, a negatively curved universe expands forever, with gravity barely slowing the rate of expansion. With dark energy, the expansion not only continues but accelerates. The ultimate fate of an open universe is either universal heat death, the "Big Freeze," or the "Big Rip," where the acceleration caused by dark energy eventually becomes so strong that it completely overwhelms the effects of the gravitational, electromagnetic and weak binding forces.

Conversely, a *negative* cosmological constant, which would correspond to a negative energy density and positive pressure, would cause even an open universe to re-collapse to a big crunch. This option has been ruled out by observations.

Flat universe

If the average density of the universe exactly equals the critical density so that $\Omega=1$, then the geometry of the universe is flat: as in Euclidean geometry, the sum of the angles of a triangle is 180 degrees and parallel lines continuously maintain the same distance.

Absent dark energy, a flat universe expands forever but at a continually decelerating rate, with expansion asymptotically approaching a fixed rate. With dark energy, the expansion rate of the universe initially slows down, due to the effect of gravity, but eventually increases. The ultimate fate of the universe is the same as an open universe.

Theories about the end of universe

The fate of the universe is determined by the density of the universe. The preponderance of evidence to date, based on measurements of the rate of expansion and the mass density, favors a universe that will continue to expand indefinitely, resulting in the "big freeze" scenario below. However new understandings of the nature of dark matter also suggest its interactions with mass and gravity demonstrate the possibility of an oscillating universe.

Big Freeze or Heat death

The Big Freeze is a scenario under which continued expansion results in a universe that asymptotically approaches absolute zero temperature. It could, in the absence of dark energy, occur only under a flat or hyperbolic geometry. With a positive cosmological constant, it could also occur in a closed universe. This scenario is currently the most commonly accepted theory within the scientific community. A related scenario is Heat death, which states that the universe goes to a state of maximum entropy in which everything is evenly distributed, and there are no gradients—which are needed to sustain information processing, one form of which is life. The Heat Death scenario is compatible with any of the three spatial models, but requires that the universe reach an eventual temperature minimum.

(end of article)

If we examine the state of the universe before the big bang, we can think of it also as being in total darkness, or in a state of nothingness. This is what the Jewish sages referred to as the "end and the beginning being one." If you wish, alpha and omega are one and the same.

The question we have now is this: who ignited this void or nothingness and was responsible for bringing it to life?

It is clear that nothingness or the one could not act on itself since it was in a totally static state. Therefore, there must have been an outside intervention that caused it to become dynamic and therefore alive.

What was this intervention?

2.3   The universe becomes dynamic

We now have the following: a universe of nothingness that is completely in static mode and is acted upon by a spiritual force from outside itself, or the one. This spiritual force has caused the universe of nothingness or the universe of absolute uniformity to become nonuniform and therefore dynamic and therefore alive.

We can conceptualize this as follows: when the spiritual force acted on the universe of nothingness or the one, it caused a completely static universe to become dynamic. It is clear that it could not have been physical, since the entire physical universe was concentrated in the one, or in the nothingness.

Because it was not of a physical nature, it could only be of (what we term) a spiritual nature.

The spiritual force caused a single point of nothingness to expand into ten dimensions and within them the lower three dimensions, thereby creating motion on the three lower physical axes of existence and in turn causing time to be born—hence, the four dimensions that we exist in and are aware of. At this point, the universe became dynamic and alive.

So far we have described four dimensions, X, Y, Z, and time, or space-time continuum. The dimension of time is just the past moving into the future where the intersection of these two entities is the present and the interaction of these four dimensions (space-time) creates our reality.

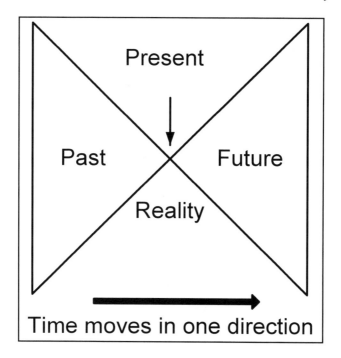

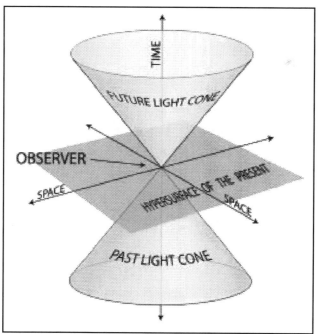

(from Wikipedia)

However, there is a fifth dimension, and that is the spiritual dimension. This fifth dimension contains a total of six other dimensions, bringing the total dimensions of the universe to ten.[8] To understand the statement mentioned above, let us review a basic outline of string theory.

For those who care to investigate further, the following may be of interest; otherwise, one can skip these equations.

Friedmann equations

(start of Wikipedia article)

The Friedmann equations are a set of equations in physical cosmology that govern the expansion of space in homogeneous and isotropic models of the universe within the context of general relativity. They were first derived by Alexander Friedmann in 1922 from Einstein's field equations of gravitation for the Friedmann-Lemaître-Robertson-Walker metric and a fluid with a given mass density ρ and pressure P. The equations for negative spatial curvature were given by Friedmann in 1924. (This section was taken from Wikipedia.org)

Assumptions

The Friedmann equations start with the simplifying assumption that the universe is spatially homogeneous and isotropic, i.e., the Cosmological Principle; empirically, this is justified on scales larger than ~100 Mpc (million parallax second). The Cosmological Principle implies that the metric of the universe must be of the form:

$$ds^2 = a(t)^2 ds_3^2 - dt^2$$

Where ds_3^2 is a three-dimensional metric that must be one of **(a)** flat space, **(b)** a sphere of constant positive curvature or **(c)** a hyperbolic space with constant negative curvature. The parameter k discussed below takes the value 0, 1, -1 in these three cases respectively. It is this fact that allows us to sensibly speak of a "scale factor" $a(t)$.

Einstein's equations now relate the evolution of this scale factor to the pressure and energy of the matter in the universe. The resulting equations are described below.

The equations

There are two independent Friedmann equations for modeling a homogeneous, isotropic universe. They are:

$$H^2 = \left(\frac{\dot{a}}{a}\right)^2 = \frac{8\pi G}{3}\rho - \frac{kc^2}{a^2} + \frac{\Lambda c^2}{3}$$

which is derived from the 00 component of Einstein's field equations, and

$$\dot{H} + H^2 = \frac{\ddot{a}}{a} = -\frac{4\pi G}{3}\left(\rho + \frac{3p}{c^2}\right) + \frac{\Lambda c^2}{3}$$

which is derived from the trace of Einstein's field equations. G, Λ, and c are universal constants (G is Newton's gravitational constant, Λ is the cosmological constant, c is the speed of light in vacuum). k is constant throughout a particular solution, but may vary from one solution to another. a, H, ρ, and p are functions of time. Where $H \equiv \dfrac{\dot{a}}{a}$, the Hubble parameter is the rate of expansion of the universe. $\dfrac{k}{a^2}$ is the spatial curvature in any time-slice of the universe; it is equal to one-sixth of the spatial Ricci curvature scalar R since $R = \dfrac{6}{a^2}(\ddot{a}a + \dot{a}^2 + kc^2)$ in the Friedmann model. There are two commonly used choices for a and k which describe the same physics:

k = +1, 0 or -1 depending on whether the shape of the universe is a closed 3-sphere, flat (i.e., Euclidean space) or an open 3-hyperboloid, respectively. If k = +1, then a is the radius of curvature of the universe. If k = 0, then a may be fixed to any arbitrary positive number at one particular time. If k = -1, then (loosely speaking) one can say that $i \cdot a$ is the radius of curvature of the universe.

a is the scale factor which is taken to be 1 at the present time. k is the spatial curvature when a = 1 (i.e. today). If the shape of the universe is hyper spherical and R_t is the radius of curvature (R_0 in the present-day), then $a = R_t / R_0$. If k is positive, then the universe is hyper spherical. If k is zero, then the universe is flat. If k is negative, then the universe is hyperbolic.

Using the first equation, the second equation can be re-expressed as

$$\dot{\rho} = -3H\left(\rho + \dfrac{p}{c^2}\right),$$

which eliminates Λ and expresses the conservation of mass-energy.

These equations are sometimes simplified by replacing

$$\rho \rightarrow \rho - \frac{\Lambda c^2}{8\pi G}$$

$$p \rightarrow p + \frac{\Lambda c^4}{8\pi G}$$

to give:

$$H^2 = \left(\frac{\dot{a}}{a}\right)^2 = \frac{8\pi G}{3}\rho - \frac{kc^2}{a^2}$$

$$\dot{H} + H^2 = \frac{\ddot{a}}{a} = -\frac{4\pi G}{3}\left(\rho + \frac{3p}{c^2}\right).$$

And the simplified form of the second equation is invariant under this transformation.

The Hubble parameter can change over time if other parts of the equation are time dependent (in particular the mass density, the vacuum energy, or the spatial curvature). Evaluating the Hubble parameter at the present time yields Hubble's constant which is the proportionality constant of Hubble's law. Applied to a fluid with a given equation of state, the Friedmann equations yield the time evolution and geometry of the universe as a function of the fluid density.

Some cosmologists call the second of these two equations the **Friedmann acceleration equation** and reserve the term *Friedmann equation* for only the first equation.

Density parameter

The density parameter, Ω, is defined as the ratio of the actual (or observed) density ρ to the critical density ρ_c of the Friedmann universe. The relation between the actual density and the critical density determines the overall geometry of the universe. In earlier models, which did not include a cosmological constant term, critical density was regarded also as the watershed between an expanding and a contracting Universe.

To date, the critical density is estimated to be approximately five atoms (of monatomic hydrogen) per cubic meter, whereas the average density of ordinary matter in the Universe is believed to be 0.2 atoms per cubic meter.[4] A much greater density comes from the unidentified dark matter; both ordinary and dark matter contribute in favor of contraction of the universe. However, the largest part comes from so-called dark energy, which accounts for the cosmological constant term. Although the total density is equal to the critical density (exactly, up to measurement error), the dark energy does not lead to contraction of the universe but rather accelerates its expansion. Therefore, the universe will expand forever.

An expression for the critical density is found by assuming Λ to be zero (as it is for all basic Friedmann universes) and setting the normalized spatial curvature, k, equal to zero. When the substitutions are applied to the first of the Friedmann equations we find:

$$\rho_c = \frac{3H^2}{8\pi G}.$$

The density parameter (useful for comparing different cosmological models) is then defined as:

$$\Omega \equiv \frac{\rho}{\rho_c} = \frac{8\pi G \rho}{3H^2}.$$

This term originally was used as a means to determine the spatial geometry of the universe, where ρ_c is the critical density for which the spatial geometry is flat (or Euclidean). Assuming a zero vacuum energy density, if Ω is larger than unity, the space sections of the universe are closed; the universe will eventually stop expanding, then collapse. If Ω is less than unity, they are open; and the universe expands forever. However, one can also subsume the spatial curvature and vacuum energy terms into a more general expression for Ω in which case this density parameter equals exactly unity. Then it is a matter of measuring the different components, usually designated by subscripts. According to the ΛCDM model, there are important components of Ω due to baryons, cold dark matter and dark energy. The spatial geometry of the universe has been measured by the WMAP spacecraft to be nearly flat. This means that the universe can be well approximated by a model where the spatial curvature parameter k is zero; however, this does not necessarily imply that the universe is infinite: it might merely be that the universe is much larger than the part we see. (Similarly, the fact that Earth is approximately flat at the scale of a region does not imply that the Earth is flat: it only implies that it is much larger than this region.)

The first Friedmann equation is often seen in a form with density parameters.

$$\frac{H^2}{H_0^2} = \Omega_R a^{-4} + \Omega_M a^{-3} + \Omega_k a^{-2} + \Omega_\Lambda.$$

Here Ω_R is the radiation density today (i.e. when $a = 1$), Ω_M is the matter (dark plus baryonic) density today, $\Omega_k = 1 - \Omega$ is the "spatial curvature density" today, and Ω_Λ is the cosmological constant or vacuum density today.

Useful solutions

The Friedmann equations can be easily solved in presence of a perfect fluid with equation of state

$$p = w\rho c^2,$$

where P is the pressure, ρ is the mass density of the fluid in the comoving frame and w is some constant. The solution for the scale factor is

$$a(t) = a_0\, t^{\frac{2}{3(w+1)}}$$

where a_0 is some integration constant to be fixed by the choice of initial conditions. This family of solutions labeled by w is extremely important for cosmology. E.g. $w = 0$ describes a matter-dominated universe, where the pressure is negligible with respect to the mass density. From the generic solution one easily sees that in a matter-dominated universe the scale factor goes as

$$a(t) \propto t^{2/3} \text{Matter-dominated}$$

Another important example is the case of a radiation-dominated universe, i.e., when $w = 1/3$. This leads to

$$a(t) \propto t^{1/2} \text{Radiation dominated}$$

Mixtures

If the matter is a mixture of two or more non-interacting fluids each with such an equation of state, then

$$\dot{\rho}_f = -3H\left(\rho_f + \frac{p_f}{c^2}\right)$$

holds separately for each such fluid f. In each case,

$$\dot{\rho}_f = -3H\left(\rho_f + w_f\rho_f\right)$$

from which we get

$$\rho_f \propto a^{-3(1+w_f)}.$$

For example, one can form a linear combination of such terms

$$\rho = Aa^{-3} + Ba^{-4} + Ca^{0}$$

where: A is the density of "dust" (ordinary matter, $w=0$) when $a=1$; B is the density of radiation ($w=1/3$) when $a=1$; and C is the density of "dark energy" ($w=-1$). One then substitutes this into

$$\left(\frac{\dot{a}}{a}\right)^{2} = \frac{8\pi G}{3}\rho - \frac{kc^2}{a^2}$$

and solves for a as a function of time.

Rescaled Friedmann equation

Set,

$$\tilde{a} = \frac{a}{a_0}, \quad \rho_c = \frac{3H_0^2}{8\pi G}, \quad \Omega = \frac{\rho}{\rho_c}, \quad t = \frac{\tilde{t}}{H_0}, \quad \Omega_c = -\frac{kc^2}{H_0^2 a_0^2}$$

$$\tilde{a} = \frac{a}{a_0}, \quad \rho_c = \frac{3H_0^2}{8\pi G}, \quad \Omega = \frac{\rho}{\rho_c}, \quad t = \frac{\tilde{t}}{H_0}, \quad \Omega_c = -\frac{kc^2}{H_0^2 a_0^2}$$

where a_0 and H_0 are separately the scale factor and the Hubble parameter today. Then we can have

$$\frac{1}{2}\left(\frac{d\tilde{a}}{d\tilde{t}}\right)^{2} + U_{\text{eff}}(\tilde{a}) = \frac{1}{2}\Omega_c$$

Where $U_{\text{eff}}(\tilde{a}) = \dfrac{\Omega \tilde{a}^2}{2}$.

For any form of the effective potential $U_{\text{eff}}(\tilde{a})$, there is an equation of state $p = p\,(\rho)$ that will produce it.

(end of article)

2.4 Very short review of string theory

(start of article from Wikipedia)

String theory is a developing theory in <u>particle physics</u> that attempts to reconcile <u>quantum mechanics</u> and general relativity. String theory mainly posits that the <u>electrons</u> and <u>quarks</u> within an atom are not 0-dimensional objects, but rather 1-dimensional oscillating lines ("strings"), possessing only the dimension of length, but not height or width. The theory poses that these strings can vibrate, thus giving the observed particles their <u>flavor</u>, charge, <u>mass</u> and <u>spin</u>. The earliest string model, the bosonic string, incorporated only <u>bosons</u>, although this view developed to the superstring theory, which posits that a connection (a "super symmetry") exists between <u>bosons</u> and <u>fermions</u>, two fundamentally different types of particles. String theories also require the existence of several extra, unobservable, dimensions to the universe, in addition to the usual three spatial dimensions (height, width, and length) and the fourth dimension of time. M theory, for example, requires that space-time have eleven dimensions.

The theory has its origins in the dual resonance model—first proposed in 1969 by Gabriele Veneziano—which described the strongly interacting hadrons as strings. Since that time, the term *string theory* has developed to incorporate any of a group of related superstring theories. Indeed, the "strings" are no longer considered fundamental to the theory, which can also be formulated in terms of points or <u>surfaces</u>. As such, five major string theories were developed, each with a different mathematical structure, and each best describing different physical circumstances. The main differences between each theory were principally the number of dimensions in which the strings developed, and their characteristics (some were open loops, some were closed loops, etc.), however all these theories appeared to be correct. In the mid 1990s, string theorist Edward Witten of the Institute for Advanced Study considered that the five major versions of string theory might be describing the same phenomenon from different perspectives. Witten's resulting M-theory, a proposed unification of all previous superstring theories, asserted that strings are really 1-dimensional slices of a 2-dimensional membrane vibrating in 11-dimensional space. As a result of the many properties and principles shared by these approaches (such as the holographic principle), their mutual logical consistency, and the fact that some easily include the standard model of particle physics, many of the world's greatest living physicists (such as Edward Witten, Juan Maldacena and Leonard Susskind) believe that string theory is a step towards the correct fundamental description of nature. In particular, string theory is the first candidate for the theory of everything (TOE), a manner of describing the known fundamental forces (gravitational, electromagnetic, weak and strong interactions) and matter (quarks and leptons) in a mathematically complete system. However, prominent physicists such as Richard Feynman and Sheldon Lee Glashow have criticized string theory for not providing any quantitative experimental predictions. Like any other quantum theory of gravity, it is widely believed that testing the theory directly would require prohibitively expensive feats of engineering. Although direct experimental testing of String Theory involves grand explorations and development in engineering, there are several indirect experiments that may prove partial truth to String Theory. Super symmetry (an idea developed in the early 1970s through String Theory research) is theoretically established through String Theory and it does appear to weave into current experimentally understood High Energy Physics (Particle Physics) (Super symmetry could possibly be discovered at CERN where energies are being probed that could motivate the emergence of Supersymmetric Particles.

Also the existence of Extra Compactified Dimensions (Calabi-Yau manifold) could possibly be discovered at CERN by the permeation of a Graviton into a higher dimensional space (Membrane (M-Theory).

Number of dimensions

An intriguing feature of string theory is that it involves the prediction of extra dimensions. The number of dimensions is not fixed by any consistency criterion, but flat space time solutions do exist in the so-called "critical dimension." Cosmological solutions exist in a wider variety of dimensionalities, and these different dimensions—more precisely different values of the "effective central charge," a count of degrees of freedom which reduces to dimensionality in weakly curved regimes—are related by dynamical transitions.

One such theory is the 11-dimensional M-theory, which requires space time to have eleven dimensions, as opposed to the usual three spatial dimensions and the fourth dimension of time. The original string theories from the 1980s describe special cases of M-theory where the eleventh dimension is a very small circle or a line, and if these formulations are considered as fundamental, then string theory requires ten dimensions. But the theory also describes universes like ours, with four observable spacetime dimensions, as well as universes with up to 10 flat space dimensions, and also cases where the position in some of the dimensions is not described by a real number, but by a completely different type of mathematical quantity. So the notion of space-time dimension is not fixed in string theory: it is best thought of as different in different circumstances.

Nothing in Maxwell's theory of electromagnetism or Einstein's theory of relativity makes this kind of prediction; these theories require physicists to insert the number of dimensions "by both hands," and this number is fixed and independent of potential energy. String theory allows one to relate the number of dimensions to scalar potential energy. Technically, this happens because a gauge anomaly exists for every separate number of predicted dimensions, and the gauge anomaly can be counteracted by including nontrivial potential energy into equations to solve motion. Furthermore, the absence of potential energy in the "critical dimension" explains why flat space time solutions are possible.

This can be better understood by noting that a photon included in a consistent theory (technically, a particle carrying a force related to an unbroken gauge symmetry) must be massless. The mass of the photon which is predicted by string theory depends on the energy of the string mode which represents the photon. This energy includes a contribution from the Casimir effect, namely from quantum fluctuations in the string. The size of this contribution depends on the number of dimensions since for a larger number of dimensions; there are more possible fluctuations in the string position. Therefore, the photon in flat space time will be massless—and the theory consistent—only for a particular number of dimensions.

When the calculation is done, the critical dimensionality is not four as one may expect (three axes of space and one of time). The subset of X is equal to the relation of photon fluctuations in a linear dimension. Flat space string theories are 26-dimensional in the bosonic case, while superstring and M-theories turn out to involve 10 or 11 dimensions for flat solutions. In bosonic string theories, the 26 dimensions come from the Polyakov equation. Starting from any dimension greater than four, it is necessary to consider how these are reduced to four dimensional space time.

(end of article)

2.5 The expansion of the universe into ten dimensions

Article by Mr. Virgil Renzulli of Prof. Brian Greene theory.

(start of an article in the *Columbia University Record* by Brian Greene)

Physicists have spent much of the 20th century answering three major questions and redefining space and time in ways that contradict human intuition.

The three questions, all of which deal with the nature of the universe, are:

- Why can't you run away from a light beam and diminish its approach speed?

- If the sun were to explode, would you feel the gravitational impact on the Earth's orbit before you saw the explosion eight minutes later?

- Why are the two major theories in physics—one dealing with stars and galaxies, the other with atoms and subatomic particles, both proved time and time again—mutually incompatible?

The answers to these questions have not been easy for physicists to find or for lay people to comprehend. Albert

Einstein demonstrated that time slows at great speeds and that space is warped. The current "master theory" of particle physics holds that all matter is composed of tiny vibrating strings, which is easier to accept than the theory's requirement that there need to be at least six more spatial dimensions in addition to time and the three spatial dimensions that we can perceive.

String theory requires at least six extra spatial dimensions tightly curled-up to microscopic size. Here we see two such dimensions, curled-up into tiny spheres.

The question of how there can be at least 10 dimensions and probably 11 dimensions when there only appear to be four was one of the issues explored by Professor of Mathematics and Physics Brian Greene in a Graduate School of Arts and Sciences' Dean's Distinguished Lecture, "Space And Time Since Einstein," delivered Mar. 12 at the University Club. Greene, who is also writing a book on the subject, *The Elegant Universe,* to be published in January 1999 by W.W. Norton, described the three central conflicts that have driven physics in the 20th century.

The first conflict, which concerns motion and the speed of light, arose in the early 1900s. When an ordinary object such as a baseball or snowball is thrown at us, we can run away from it, causing the speed with which it approaches us to decrease. But if you try to run away from a beam of light, you cannot make it approach you any slower.

"Light will always approach you at 186,000 miles per second whether you run away from it, run toward it or stand still," said Greene. "Einstein resolved the paradox by showing that our intuition regarding space and time was wrong, that our conception of motion—the distance something travels divided by the time it takes to get there—was incorrect."

Einstein's Special Theory of Relativity explained that the speed of light is a constant and that at great speeds, time slows down (relatively speaking) and space becomes distorted.

But in solving the paradox, Einstein came into conflict with another towering figure of physics, Isaac Newton and his Theory of Gravity, which holds that the gravitational force is transmitted instantaneously—or faster than the speed of light.

"If the sun were to explode," said Greene, "we would not know about it visually for eight minutes because it would take eight minutes for light from the explosion to reach us from the sun. According to Newton, however, the gravitational disturbance would immediately cause our orbit to abruptly change. So, the influence of gravity, in Newton's Theory, is transmitted much faster than light. Einstein knew that nothing could exceed the light speed, and for the next decade he struggled to resolve this conflict.

"His answer is the General Theory of Relativity, by which he showed us how gravity is transmitted through the warping of space, and if you look closely at how the space warps travel, much like ripples in a pond, you find they travel at light speed. And so, gravity is transmitted at exactly the same speed as light.

"In actuality, then, if the sun were to explode, we would not know about it immediately by an abrupt change in our orbital motion. Instead, exactly when we saw the explosion, we would feel it."

WHAT MATTER IS MADE OF—As explained by Brian Greene, above, all matter consists of atoms which are themselves composed of electrons swarming around a central nucleus. String theory adds a new ultramicroscopic layer by declaring that subatomic particles actually consist of tiny loops of vibrating energy, "strings."

Einstein's General Theory of Relativity, which is applicable to things very big—gravity, stars, galaxies—became one of the two pillars upon which 20th century physics is based. The second pillar is Quantum Mechanics, which describes the microscopic structure of the world—atoms and subatomic particles.

"Each of these pillars has been tested for accuracy," said Greene. "Each comes through with flying colors, and yet, the two theories are mutually incompatible. And that has been the driving conflict in physics for the last half century.

"The heart of Quantum Mechanics is summarized by (Werner) Heisenberg's Uncertainty Principal and that tells us that there are certain

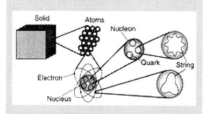

features of the microscopic world that we cannot know with total precision. It's not a limit of technology; there are just some complimentary things we can't know simultaneously.

"For example, Heisenberg showed us that when you look at smaller and smaller regions of space, the amount of energy embodied in that space is known with less and less precision. There is a tremendous amount of roiling, hot, kinetic energy bound up in every little morsel of space and the smaller the morsel the more the energy.

"If you've got a lot of energy in tiny distances, it means that space is incredibly frothy and wildly undulating, and these undulations are so violent that they completely destroy Einstein's Geometrical Model of Space, the central principle of General Relativity. On large scales, such as that of galaxies and beyond, these microscopic kinetic undulations average out to zero; we don't see them. Only when we focus on microscopic distances, do we become aware of the tumult that is going on and realize that it is so severe that Einstein's theory falls apart."

The conflict continued for half a century until the development of Super String Theory, which reconciles Quantum Mechanics with the General Theory of Relativity.

"If you examine microscopic particles the way people did in the early part of the century, you come to the conclusion that the elementary constituents of nature are little dots that have no further internal structures," explained Greene. "String Theory tells us that if you were to probe inside these dots with a precision not possible with our present technology, you would find each has a little vibrating loop, a vibrating filament of energy, inside of it. And the difference between one particle of matter and another, according to Super String Theory, is the pattern of vibration that the string is undergoing. Different particles can be compared to different notes that an ordinary vibrating violin string can play—electrons, photons, quarks.

"String Theory also holds that there is a smallest possible distance in the world, the size of the string. And this distance is just large enough that the pernicious small scale quantum undulations predicted by Heisenberg's Uncertainty Principle are avoided. Some people feel cheated with this explanation. What it means is that the problem we thought was there was not there at all."

String Theory may also lead to a Unified Theory in which all the principles and theories of physics can be distilled into a single overarching statement. String Theory holds that absolutely everything is a manifestation of a single object—a string. When it vibrates one way, it looks like an electron. When it vibrates another way, it looks like a photon. All the particles and all the forces are part of a single unified concept. "Super String Theory has its own remaking of space-time," said Greene. "It requires that it have more than three space dimensions."

If strings can only vibrate north and south, east and west, up and down, there are not enough variations to account for all the particles and forces. The equations of String Theory require at least six more spatial dimensions.

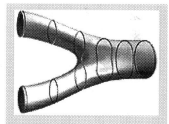

STRINGS IN ACTION—Two string loops interact by joining together into a third string.

Greene used an example of a garden hose to explain why we don't see these additional dimensions. From a distance, the hose looks like a straight line, and if an ant lived on the hose, it could move up and down its length.

But if you move closer to the hose, you realize it has another dimension, its girth, and the ant could walk around the hose as well.

Dimensions, therefore, would come in two types: those that are long and visible and those that are tiny and curled up, existing only on the microscopic level of strings.

"String Theory has the capacity to describe not only how the universe is, but how it got to be the way it is," said Greene. "It may give us an explanation of why there is space and why there is time. In the same way that cloth is made of thread woven together in a pattern, some theorists have suggested that strings themselves are the threads of space and time. Space and time themselves may be the result of an enormous number of little vibrating strings all coalescing together and vibrating in a particular coherent pattern.

"If so, you can imagine a state of the universe when the strings have not coalesced in that manner, and space and time have not yet been formed. And it is possible that the universe could return to that state."

Could strings also coalesce into another kind of universe?

"In principle," said Greene, "it is possible." (End of article)

2.6 Quantum mechanics and the Heisenberg principle of uncertainty

Uncertainty principle

(start of article from Wikipedia)

In quantum mechanics, the **Heisenberg uncertainty principle,**
$$\Delta x \, \Delta p \geq \frac{\hbar}{2}$$ states by precise inequalities that certain pairs

of physical properties, such as position and momentum, cannot be simultaneously known to arbitrarily high precision. That is, the more precisely one property is measured, the less precisely the other can be measured. The principle states that a minimum exists for the product of the uncertainties in these properties that is equal to or greater than one half of the reduced Planck's constant ($\hbar = h/2\pi$).

Published by Werner Heisenberg in 1927, the principle means that it is impossible to *determine* simultaneously both the position and velocity of an electron or any other particle with any great degree of accuracy or certainty. Moreover, his principle is not a statement about the limitations of a researcher's ability to measure particular quantities of a system, but it is a statement about *the nature of the system itself* as described by the equations of quantum mechanics.

(end of article)

2.7   Life cycle of the universe

Because there is a beginning and an end, there must be a life cycle to the universe. This life cycle is measured in billions of years. Science does not have an accurate answer yet about when the universe will end. Stephen Hawking's estimates for a cold universe (discussed below) is 10^{72} years. However, other scientists believe that it might be as long as 10^{500}.

Ultimate fate of the universe

(start of article from Wikipedia)

Big Freeze or Heat death

The Big Freeze is a scenario under which continued expansion results in a universe that asymptotically approaches absolute zero temperature. It could, in the absence of dark energy, occur only under a flat or hyperbolic geometry. With a positive cosmological constant, it could also occur in a closed universe. This scenario is currently the most commonly accepted theory within the scientific community. A related scenario is Heat death, which states that the universe goes to a state of maximum entropy in which everything is evenly distributed, and there are no gradients—which are needed to sustain information processing, one form of which is life. The Heat Death scenario is compatible with any of the three spatial models, but requires that the universe reach an eventual temperature minimum.

(end of article)

Chapter 3   Biblical Account of Creation

The biblical account of creation is a top-down account. It is best explained through analogy.

Suppose a person decides to build a house. What is the process that he must go through to build it?

Obviously, the first thing is the will to build a house; in other words, he must want to build a house. The second step is finding an appropriate site or appropriate land for such a house. The third is to design an architectural plan for the house, which requires knowledge. The fourth is to develop the site for such a house, in other words, moving earth, rocks, and trees, draining water if necessary, and so on, from the site where the house is going to be built. The fifth step is to assemble all the materials needed for the construction of this house at the building site. The sixth is to pour the foundation. The seventh is to hire tradesmen (carpenters, electricians, plumbers, masons, painters, and so on) to build the house.

It is clear that the above description of building a house is a top-down account. In such an account, the actual builders of the house and any people involved in each stage of its development know their task and how the house must be built. In other words, once the architectural plans are designed and available, a total understanding of what the house will look like is immediately clear before any effort is invested in building it.

The architect of such a house does not need to know exactly where each nail is driven into a specific beam as long as the beam is in the right place and is properly secured to carry whatever load it is designed to carry.

Anyone desiring to see the house and to understand its scope in terms of number of rooms, location of doors, windows, steps, room heights, and so on can easily look at the architectural plans for such a purpose.

Therefore, looking at creation from a top-down viewpoint provides an immediate or reasonably quick understanding of the total creation without the need to know every detail.

On the other hand, a bottom-up scenario of building such a house is much more complicated. Suppose we want to build the same house and give our tradesmen nails, electrical cord, pipes, and materials but don't have architectural plans to give them. How are they going to build this house?

Obviously, they will be able to construct only small pieces of a wall or a window, dig a tunnel for some pipes, and so on, but they will have no idea what this house should look like. The analogy here is similar to our scientists who construct theories, discover physical laws, and are able to construct pieces of the overall architectural plan of the universe (a house, in our analogy).

To this end of describing the top-down scenario of creation, we consider the following:

3.1 Top-down biblical account of creation—God and his creation

Initial conditions of the universe (as discussed in previous sections):

1. Nothingness is the universe of absolute uniformity.
2. The universe of absolute uniformity is one.
3. The beginning and the end are the same.
4. The beginning and the end are nothingness.
5. The one is physical entity.
6. The one (universe) expands into ten dimensions.

We now have the following equations:

I.   Nothingness = Absolute uniformity = One (conditions 1 and 2)

II.   one = {universe} = one (conditions 3, 4, 5, and 6)

If: Universe = U, and sum (U) = ΣU is taken over its ten dimensions from 1 to 10, then

III.   One $\rightarrow$ {U} $\rightarrow$ Σ U $\rightarrow$ near or $=\infty$ $\rightarrow$ One

{Nothingness} $\rightarrow$ {Big bang} $\rightarrow$ {Expansion phase} $\rightarrow$ {Decay}

            Birth   Life   Death

IV.   Universal life cycle = Σ all three phases from initial ignition to total darkness

In equation III., the near or equal infinity sign means that all ten dimensions of the universe decay at a level near or equal to infinity.

Equation IV. says that the universal life cycle is the universe evolving from an initial single point of nothingness to an expansion that is the universe itself made of ten dimensions, that decays into nothingness again at the end of all ten dimensions, not only of time.

For those who are interested, the Randall-Sundrum model of extra dimensions is shown below; however, one can skip these equations and continue with the text.

Randall–Sundrum model

(start of article from Wikipedia)

The RS1 model

The RS1 model attempts to address the hierarchy problem. The warping of the extra dimension is analogous to the warping of space time in the vicinity of a massive object, such as a black hole. This warping, or red-shifting, generates a large ratio of energy scales so that the natural energy scale at one end of the extra dimension is much larger than at the other end.

$$ds^2 = \frac{1}{k^2 y^2}(dy^2 + \eta_{\mu\nu}\, dx^\mu\, dx^\nu)$$

where k is some constant and η has "-+++" metric signature.

This space has boundaries at $y = 1/k$ and $y = 1/Wk$, with $0 \le \frac{1}{k} \le \frac{1}{Wk}$ where k is around the Planck scale and W is the warp factor and Wk is around a TeV. The boundary at $y = 1/k$ is called the **Planck brane** and the boundary at $y = 1/Wk$ is called the **TeV brane**. The particles of the standard model reside on the TeV brane. The distance between both branes is only $-\ln (W)/k$, though.

In another coordinate system,

$$\varphi \overset{\text{def}}{=} -\frac{\pi \ln(ky)}{\ln(W)},$$

so that

$$0 \leq \varphi \leq \pi$$

and

$$ds^2 = \left(\frac{\ln(W)}{\pi k}\right)^2 d\varphi^2 + e^{\frac{2\ln(W)\varphi}{\pi}} \eta_{\mu\nu} \, dx^\mu \, dx^\nu.$$

(end of article)

3.2 Creation: Genesis 1 and 2

Genesis 1:2 says that the Earth was void and without any form (תהו ובהו), and there was darkness upon the deep. What is meant here is that the universe did not exist yet and was not formed. It further says that the spirit of God was hovering over the water. This means that there were two entities, the entity of nothingness or the one, and the spiritual entity that acted on it as was discussed earlier. We have used dark universe in science and water in our analogy earlier in the book to explain nothingness and absolute uniformity.

Consider the Hebrew words תהו ובהו. The meaning of the words תהו ובהו can now be understood as nothingness, as was discussed earlier. Note that the Old Testament begins with the letter ב or *B* of the Hebrew alphabet, whereas the letter ת or *T* is the last letter of the five books of

Moses and also the last letter of the Hebrew alphabet. What is meant here is that one universal cycle has just ended and become nothingness, and it is time to start the cycle again. One typically starts a new cycle after the end of an existing cycle.

Genesis 1:3 says, "God said let there be light, and there was light." The light that God commanded upon the universe of nothingness is not physical but rather spiritual light.

Genesis 1:3 says, "Let there be light." In Hebrew it is shown as two words having three letters each.

יְהִי אוֹר, , which can be read as יְהַ. יְ אוֹר

The first word can be broken into two: *Yah* (made up of *Yod* and *Hei*), and *Yod* as shown above (יה ?). This means God and the ten sefirot. Since the first two letters are *God* in Hebrew, and the *Yod* by itself represents the numerical value of ten, or the ten sefirot (the ten sefirot are all that there is within the living universe), they can be thought of as emanations or the ten dimensions of the universe discussed earlier. The second word is *OR*, אוֹר which is made up of *aleph, vav,* and *reish,* meaning "light."

These two Hebrew words are saying that God light created the ten sefirot (the subject of the sefirot is complex and will be covered here only briefly; for more information please refer to *Sefer Yetzirah* by Rabbi Aryeh Kaplan), which make up the existing universe. It is now clear that it was God's light or infinite mind that ignited the one and injected consciousness into the one.

Let us examine this process of creation based on our initial conditions of the universe.

If a perturbation is introduced into the universe of absolute uniformity, or into the one, which is in a static state, then a non-uniform state will occur, and a dynamic state will result.

The introduction of a perturbation will create a wave that will continue until it completes its cycle, and then it will return to its original state or nothingness, or one, a static state again.

Before the "big bang," the universe was made of absolute uniformity, having one dimension and being one, completely static.

Creation started when a perturbation was introduced into the one. This is the "big bang," which caused a single point in the one, or in the universe of absolute uniformity, or nothingness, to change from a single point of one dimension into a universe of ten dimensions, causing the one to be in the dynamic state.

The expansion forward of particles or energy in all these ten dimensions has caused the lower three dimensions to come into existence as physical entities (a process of filtering or thickening). Since all the ten dimensions are bounded as one, the fourth dimension, being time, has come into existence as a continuum on which the lower three dimensions are projected.

This perturbation has created all that exists in this universe through the unfolding of the universal life wave cycle. The one became all. This means that every event in the universe was playing out at this stage on the continuum of time. Note here that both Buddha and Jesus have used this notion with their hand symbols, as shown below.

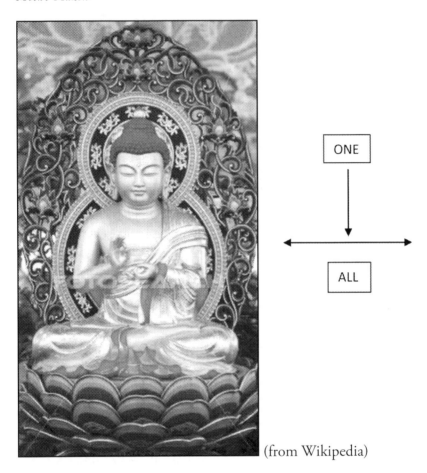

(from Wikipedia)

Buddha is shown here with the index finger and right thumb touching each other, and the position of the vertical right hand over the horizontally positioned receiving open left hand, which also has the index finger and the thumb touching each other. The meaning of this posture is as follows: the top of the index finger of the right hand symbolizes peace, and the upper segment of the thumb symbolizes joy and tranquility. The message is clear: may peace, joy, and tranquility descend from the one into all mankind. Jesus used similar hand symbols; however, he is shown in both the above-mentioned posture and with the right-hand ring finger touching the thumb. When Jesus is shown in the same posture as the one shown above, the meaning is the same as with Buddha. However, when he used the ring finger and the thumb, he meant to say that beauty and charm may descend from the one into all mankind. It is mistakenly thought to symbolize the sign of the cross.

(from Wikipedia)

Creation is therefore the combination of particles or energy units generated after the "big bang," possibly the photon, into more complex dynamic structures galaxies, stars, planets, and organic life itself that are played on the continuum of time.

Let us now examine the transformation of the universe into its ten dimensions from the top-down biblical point of view. This process parallels the scientific explanation of the universe into its ten dimensions as discussed in chapter 2.5 above.

3.3   The Tree of Life

The biblical Tree of Life is thought to be made of the entire ten sefirot or emanations, which parallel the transformation of the universe into its ten dimensions. The traditional representation of the Tree of Life is shown below.

Traditional ten sefirot

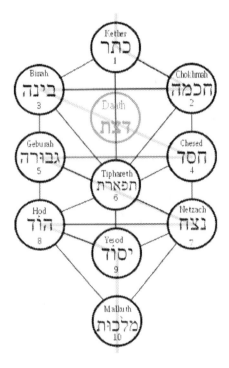

These ten sefirot represent various levels of existence. The highest level is the level of will, which also is called Crown. I have derived these ten emanations from a viewpoint that is different from the traditional approach.

Please note that the essence of the ten sefirot is the same in the following derivations as with the traditional method; however, the meaning is different from the traditional thoughts for some of these dimensions.

3.4   The ten sefirot

1. Because the static state of one has changed into a dynamic state of motion and energy, it led to the formation of a ten-dimensional universe where the lower three dimensions are our width, length, and height (x, y, z), and the fourth dimension is time (t). This is our space-time continuum. A single point of nothingness exploded into these ten dimensions, which created space and time as we now know it. However, there is a fifth dimension, which includes the remaining six dimensions within it, similar to an onion with its many layers. These dimensions are discussed below.

2. Because life can exist only within a living environment, it means that the universe itself became alive from the first instance of the introduction of the perturbation, or the event of the "big bang" explosion. The universe became dynamic and therefore alive.

3. Because the beginning and the end are of the same state, completely static, the universe will return to the state of absolute uniformity, or, in our perception, it will die. All will become one again, meaning that the entire universe will become nothingness again and therefore one.

4. Because the universe is alive, it has a consciousness or a mind.

Where did this mind originate? Static matter by itself, such as the one, has no mind by itself. The mind therefore must be from outside of it. We call this mind the infinite mind, or God. This is supported in the first chapter of Genesis by the intelligent process of creation as we will see shortly.

5. The conscious mind that was injected into the universe contained infinite knowledge.
6. Knowledge contains both good and evil. It is clear that if one is taught how to build a specific item, he is also immediately taught how to destroy it. Therefore, knowledge has two sides that are inseparable and of the same entity.
7. These two sides of knowledge are the creator and the destroyer. They are exact opposites. One can't exist without the other in the universe of knowledge.

For the creator to create without the destroyer destroying everything that was created, they must be separated as long as the universal life cycle exists. This is evident in all structures in the universe, including the atomic structures of matter where the proton (positive) and the electron (negative) are separated by a distance, or the matter and antimatter, which must be separated. Otherwise, they would annihilate each other and the universe of matter could not exist.

8. For the two sides of knowledge to exist at the same universe they must be separated by the sixth dimension from the top or the fifth dimension from the bottom. We call this dimension beauty. Below this dimension, our physical universe can be observed.
9. The fourth dimension from the bottom is the continuum of time.

Time

(start of article from Wikipedia)

Time has been defined as the continuum in which events occur in succession from the past to the present and on to the future. Time has also been defined as a one-dimensional quantity used to sequence events, to quantify the durations of events and the intervals between them, and (used together with other quantities such as space) to quantify and measure the motions of objects and other changes. Time is quantified in comparative terms (such as longer, shorter, faster, quicker, slower) or in numerical terms using units (such as seconds, minutes, hours, days). Time has been a major subject of religion, philosophy, and science, but defining it in a non-controversial manner applicable to all fields of study has consistently eluded the greatest scholars.

Stephen Hawking in particular has addressed a connection between time and the Big Bang. In *A Brief History of Time* and elsewhere, Hawking says that even if time did not begin with the Big Bang and there were another time frame before the Big Bang, no information from events then would be accessible

(end of article)

The lower seven dimensions

Dimensions 5, 6, and 7 are the upper dimensions

Time is the 4th dimension

Time is the continuum between the lower 3 dimensions and the 5th, 6th, and 7th dimensions.

Dimensions 1, 2, and 3 are the lower physical dimensions

10. Time is the middle ground of the universe. What is meant here is that the dimension of time keeps these two opposing existences separated and acts as a curtain between them.

11. The dimension of time was born at the "big bang," and it is the power that causes the universal life cycle to unfold.

12. Time holds the universe together. It is a continuum in which all events take place. It is clear that without the dimension of time, the universe as we know it would not exist. Therefore, it is the binding force of nature, and by its existence, the universal life cycle can unfold from its beginning to its end.

13. Time moves forward in one direction from its initial state of zero to its end.

14. As time moves forward, the universal life cycle unfolds, causing the universe to age by having a portion of the universal matter converted back into nothingness (black holes).

15. The portion of the universe that was converted into nothingness does not exist any longer as a living entity; therefore, the universe does not have a past as we do. The universe has only present and future.

16. Because all life forms have life spans smaller than the universal life cycle, there exists for them another time scale where there is past, present, and future.

17. The present and future of all living entities is the same as the universal time scale of present and future. However, the past of all living entities is still the present of the living universe.

    To understand this concept, consider the life span of a mosquito, which is eighteen hours. We who have longer life spans can watch the mosquito be born, live, and die in our present time, but for the mosquito, his entire life and that of his descendants are all part of our present time.

18. There are many realities. The reality of all living entities is their present time, which is different from the living universe present time. This was discussed and shown graphically earlier.

19. Eternity is a concept that exists only for living entities. It is the time span between the living entities present and the living universe present. The time separation is in the billions and billions of years (from the smallest unit of time to eternity).

    One can think of eternity as a time unit between 10-E100 to 10+E100 seconds. This is an enormous time scale of trillionths and trillionths of a second and up to trillions and trillions of years. On this scale, eternity will be across the entire scale of time and up to its upper mathematical values.

20. The time span separating these two presents contains the memory of the universe of all things that happened in that time span of the living universe. It is not the past of the universe since that concept does not exist any longer but has vanished into nothingness.

21. The memory of the universe is storage that can be looked at through the vision of prophecy (eight sefira from the top—sort of like Read Only Memory or ROM). It is made from all ten dimensions of the universe at a specific instant of time.

The concept of prophecy can be understood as follows:

Consider that within the universe, every atom, planet, or galaxy has a known path of existence. In other words, the universe that contains all these structures knows where each one is and where it is going to be in the next instant (a deterministic view of the universe). Therefore, it can predict what is going to happen to a specific body of matter in any one instant of time, what the following paths or states of existence are for those particles if they collide with another body of matter, the state of those that result from such a collision, and so on. In short, there is an exact knowledge of the state of any particle in the universe at any given instant of time. This is the deterministic universe that Einstein strongly proposed. He said, ""Quantum mechanics is certainly imposing. But an inner voice tells me that it is not yet the real thing. The theory says a lot, but does not really bring us any closer to the secret of the 'old one.' I, at any rate, am convinced that *He* does not throw dice."

Letter from Einstein to Max Born (4 December 1926); *The Born-Einstein Letters* (translated by Irene Born), (Walker and Company, New York, 1971), ISBN 0-8027-0326-7. This quotation is commonly paraphrased "God does not play dice" or "God does not play dice with the universe," and other slight variants.

Indeed, from the top-down view of the universe, Einstein is correct. However, from our perception, which is the bottom-up view of the universe, there is a state of uncertainty summarized by the Heisenberg principle of uncertainty, as discussed earlier.

This does not mean that the universe itself does not know where each particle within it is, just that when we attempt to measure a specific particle's state of existence, we run into the realm of uncertainty because we are affecting its state of existence by our measurement, as it should be. Therefore, because the memory of the universe is the state of existence of the universe at a specific time, one can peek into it without disturbing its flow or the storage mechanism, which is the memory itself. The actual "peeking" is done on a level higher than the space-time continuum. This is necessary in order to view the entire space-time continuum as it unfolds.

Consider the following: if we want to peek at the XY plane from a point in the Z plane, we can do so without disturbing whatever is taking place in the XY plane. Similarly, if we want to "peek" at the space-time continuum from another dimension, our "peeking" will not affect the flow of the space-time continuum.

22. Prophecy is flashes (small units of time or, to use an analogy, single photographic frames) of eternity. It is not a continuous stream of information that makes up a moving picture (movie).

We can now summarize all of the above.

As discussed above, before any action or event can take place, there must be a will, which in the traditional representation of the ten sefirot is called Crown (first sefira; see the schematic shown below). The universe came into existence because God willed it. Through this will, the one was ignited and became all. This is the universe of absolute uniformity, which is transformed into all that there is. The traditional representation of this state is called Wisdom (second sefira, as shown below). Wisdom is often thought of as a single uniform entity that powers knowledge. We may say that a person is very knowledgeable, but to be wise is a stage above knowledge.

To create anything, Knowledge (third sefira as shown below) must exist. However, Knowledge has two sides: Good (fourth sefira as shown below), or the Creator (in a traditional representation of the ten sefirot it is thought of as Love or Mercy), and Destructive or Evil (fifth sefira as shown below), or the Destroyer. (In traditional representations of the ten sefirot it is thought of as Might or Power. Might, when it is concentrated in a single point, is the greatest destructive force in the universe.) The sixth sefira as viewed from the top down is the separating entity, the middle ground, the neutral zone, as was discussed earlier.

Eternity (seventh sefira as shown below) is a time scale for the soul. It is a universal memory that can be peeked into through Prophecy (eighth sefira) as was discussed earlier. In the same way that the Creator and the Destroyer were separated by the middle ground, neutral zone, Eternity and Prophecy needed to be dealt with on a common ground so that both states could be accommodated, which is the continuum of time.

Because Eternity applies only to living entities existing within the universal life cycle and means "no change," whereas Prophecy was allowed only a peek into the universal life cycle, thereby existing only for an instant, meaning "instantaneous change," existence in these higher-level dimensions does not permit life forms that are made of the three lower dimensions. The state of these higher dimensions is of energy forms, which is much purer and "earlier," before the formation of combinatorial organic or other molecules.

Viewing the universe from a top-down perspective, one can find the strong force and weak forces, the quarks, the proton, the atom, the molecule, and matter. Therefore, a Soul or astral body (ninth sefira) was created to experience the universal life cycle. The Soul or astral body can experience the universal life cycle anywhere between the smallest units of time represented in Prophecy to the time scale of infinity represented in Eternity.

When a living entity dies, only the physical body decomposes into basic elements. However, the consciousness that was discussed earlier exists on the axes of time as part of the mind and memory of the universe. This is what we call the Soul or astral body.

However, this astral body could experience the universe only from the fourth dimension of Time to the tenth dimension of Will. The top six dimensions are all included in the "light of God" as was discussed earlier. We call the light of God spirituality. Therefore, to partake fully in the universal life cycle, which includes the lower four dimensions (height, length, width, time) or space-time as we call it, a Physical Body (tenth sefira as shown below) was necessary.

On planet Earth, physical human bodies were created that included both man and woman, and they were called Adam, meaning "creatures of earth." These two humans were kept in an environment (the Garden of Eden, which was not subject to aging as we know it).

It is possible that other beings were created on other planets for the same purpose. It should be noted that earlier organic life forms were created on planet Earth, all of which have some kind of astral bodies or souls. However, only Adam was created to experience the entire creation, on Earth and beyond. We can now derive a graphical representation of all the above discussion of the ten sefirot or ten dimensions of the universe. This graphical representation is shown below.

The parallel between the biblical text of Genesis and our concepts of advanced physics as we know it today is shown in the text boxes within the diagram shown below. Note that the light in Genesis 1:3 represents the original light injected into nothingness or into the dimension of absolute uniformity or the darkness that existed at that point and lacking any kind of energy. Once that happened (big bang), the universe came into existence and the other dimensions evolved.

The separation between "light" and "darkness" takes place at the same instance that the big bang occurs. This is represented in Genesis 1:4 and on the diagram below as the connections between the third dimension to the fourth and fifth. Once that takes place, a balance must be established, which is the sixth dimension as shown below. The establishment of this balance is done at the same instance that light and darkness are created. Time, which is created at that same instance, is the seventh dimension from the top.

Time, however, includes within it both dimensions of Eternity, which is the seventh dimension representing such a large time scale that it can be considered Eternity, and the eighth dimension, which contains the smallest unit of time and as such can be considered as flashes or single frames of a continuous movie and is referred to as Prophecy.

The last two dimensions include the "thickening" or the formation of various energy particles created from the big bang into atomic structures and into molecules and various forms of matter.

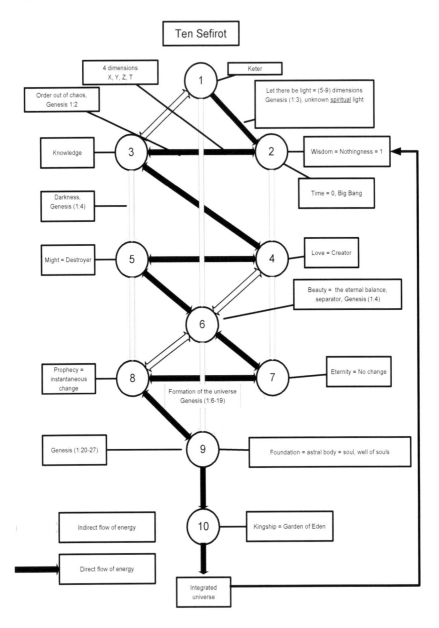

Ten Sefirot

4 dimensions
X, Y, Z, T

Keter

Order out of chaos,
Genesis 1:2

Let there be light = (5-9) dimensions
Genesis (1:3), unknown spiritual light

Knowledge

Wisdom = Nothingness = 1

Darkness,
Genesis (1:4)

Time = 0, Big Bang

Might = Destroyer

Love = Creator

Beauty = the eternal balance,
separator, Genesis (1:4)

Prophecy =
instantaneous
change

Eternity = No change

Formation of the universe
Genesis (1:6-19)

Genesis (1:20-27)

Foundation = astral body = soul, well of souls

Indirect flow of energy

Kingship = Garden of Eden

Direct flow of energy

Integrated
universe

3.5 Terraforming of planet Earth

After the formation of matter in the universe and the existence of planet Earth in its pre-formed state, God proceeds to prepare the planet for life forms (terraforming).

On the second day, in Genesis 1:6, God creates the atmosphere. In Genesis 1:7, God separates the water that is above the oceans from the water that is in the oceans below the atmosphere.

On the third day, in Genesis 1:9, God causes the land to show up (by freezing the water over the Earth's poles), and in Genesis 1:11, God seeds the Earth that is now exposed to the sun with grass, all kinds of trees, and all kinds of vegetation.

On the fourth day, in Genesis 1:16, God creates the sun, the moon, and all the stars of heaven.

This is why the early theologians thought Earth was at the center of the universe. This is because of the process of creation given in Genesis: Earth's land was exposed first and seeded with grass, trees, and all kind of vegetation, and only afterward did God create the sun, moon, and stars. This means that Earth's vegetation did not use the rays of the sun to grow.

This causes a problem in our understanding of the process of nature for the growth of grass and plants. However, one must note that there was light already in the universe (nebula) and over the Earth, but not necessarily in a concentrated form as the sun is today or the moon is today. Therefore, the grass and the plants could indeed grow under these conditions, provided there was sufficient water in the atmosphere (Genesis 2:6).

On the fifth day, in Genesis 1:20 and 1:21, God creates life in the water. On the sixth day, God creates all the animal life on the land, according to Genesis 1:24.

On the sixth day, in Genesis 1:26, God says, "Let us make Adam in our image and in our likeness." The text in Genesis continues in verse

27 by saying that "God created Adam in his image and in his likeness, male and female he created them."

3.6 Mankind

The human body of Adam was created from the materials found on Earth, as mentioned in Genesis 2:7. The word *Adam* comes from *Adama,* which is "earth." Adam, the human body of both male and female, was fashioned from the ten sefirot as shown in the table below. Note that we can find similarities between several major religions, such as Judaism, Hinduism, Muslims, Christianity, and others as shown below.

(from occult-advances.org)

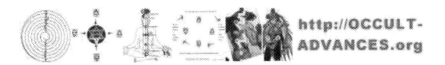

N°	Psychological functions, Symbolism	Chakra	Physiological functions	Sephira	Planet	Metal
10	Spirituality = completion = 10	Crown (Sahasrara)	Pineal gland; regulates night and day	Kether	1st Swirling	---
9	Imagination, Artistic abilities, art = closest to completion = 9	Yin Chandra Ajna area	Thalamic area, helps pituitary gland	Chokmah	Zodiac	---
8	Rationality = structures = cubic = 8 corners	Yang Surya: Ajna area	Pituitary gland, controls other glands	Binah	Saturn	lead
7	Justice = law of God = 7	Yin Visuddha	Throat	Geburah	Jupiter	tin

6	Ego, communication = 6	Yang Visuddha	To speak, mouth	Chesed	Mars	iron
5	Love, Openness = Humanity = 5	Heart: Anahata	Heart, circulatory system, blood	Tiphareth	Sun	gold
4	Control of emotions Social abilities = stability = 4	Yin: Navel	Digestive system: 2nd phase assimilation,	Hod	Venus	copper
3	Work = Business = masonry = 3	Yang: Solar Plexus: Manipura	Digestive system: 1st phase: digestion	Netzach	Mercury	mercury
2	Sexual energy = 1+1 = 2	Sex Swadhistana	Reproductive organs	Yesod	Moon	silver
1	Physical energy, will to live, survival = basis = 1	Root Mulhadara	Spinal column, Adrenal	Malkuth	Earth	---

(start of article from Wikipedia)

Comparisons with Esoteric Traditions

Chakra is a concept referring to wheel-like vortices which, according to traditional Indian medicine, are believed to exist in the surface of the etheric double of man. The Chakras are said to be "force centers" or whorls of energy permeating, from a point on the physical body, the layers of the subtle bodies in an ever-increasing fan-shaped formation. Rotating vortices of subtle matter, they are considered the focal points for the reception and transmission of energies. Different systems posit a varying number of chakras, the most well known system in the West is that of 7 chakras.

It is typical for chakras to be depicted as either flower-like or wheel-like. In the former, a specific number of "petals" are shown around the perimeter of a circle. In the latter, a certain number of spokes divide the circle into segments that make the chakra resemble a wheel (or "chakra"). Each chakra possesses a specific number of segments or petals.

A number of other mystical traditions talk about subtle energies that flow through the body, and identify specific parts of the body as being subtle centers. There are many similarities between systems, however, none of these traditions developed in isolation; the Indian mystical traditions had contact with the Chinese and Islamic mystical traditions, and they may have mutually influenced one another. Similarly, the Jewish and Islamic mystical traditions shared a great deal in common, especially during the Islamic occupation of Spain, and Jewish mysticism in particular had influence over Christian mysticism.

Qigong, the Dantian

Qigong also relies on a similar model of the human body as an energy system, except that it involves the circulation of qi (ki, chi) energy. The Qi energy, equivalent to the Hindu Prana, flows through the energy channels called channel, equivalent to the nadis, but 2 other energies are also important, Jing, the sexual energy, and Shen, or spirit energy.

In the principle circuit of qi, called the Microcosmic orbit, energy rises up a main meridian along the spine, but also comes back down the front torso. Throughout its cycle it enters various dan tian (elixir fields) which act as furnaces, where the types of energy in the body (jing, qi and shen) are progressively refined. These Dantians play a very similar role to that of chakras. The number of Dantians varies depending on the system; the navel dantian is the most well-known (it is called the Hara in Japan), but there is usually a Dantian located at the heart and between the eyebrows. The lower dantian at or below the navel transforms sexual essence, or jing, into qi energy. The middle dantian in the middle of the chest transforms qi energy into shen, or spirit, and the higher dantian at the level of the forehead (or at the top of the head), transforms Shen into wuji, infinite space of void.

In Japan, the word *qi* is written "ki," and is related to the practice of Reiki, and plays an important role in Japanese martial arts such as Aikido.

Sufism, the Lataif

Many Sufi orders make use of Lata'if, subtle centers in the body which are between 4 or 7 in number, and relate to ever more subtle levels of intimacy with Allah. But although some Lataif correspond in position to the chakras, there are also some big differences in position and meaning.

One 6 lata'if system positions the nafs, or lower self, below the navel, the qalb, or heart, in the left of the chest, the ruh, or spirit, to the right of the chest, the sirr, or secret, in the solar plexus, the khafi, or latent subtlety, in the position of the third eye, and the Akhfa, or most arcane, at the top of the head. They are frequently associated with a color, as well as a particular prophet.

Unlike the Indian and Chinese system, the emphasis is not upon these subtle centers performing a kind of inner alchemy upon the energies of the body, such as kundalini awakening, and they are not considered like organs for the subtle body; instead, they represent more abstract, philosophical concepts, representing ever greater degrees of closeness to Allah.

Kabbalah, the Sephiroth

The Jewish mystical tradition known as kabbalah often makes use of the Tree of Life, which rises up in 3 columns, and upon which are placed 10 sephiroth, occupying 7 levels. These are often associated with parts of the body, notably Malkuth and

Yesod with the genitals, Tifaret with the heart, and Kether with the crown of the head, which are located upon the central pillar. However, like the Sufi systems described above, the function of the Sephiroth is not as organs within a subtle body, instead they represent the power of Yahweh made manifest in the world, and the ascent of the Tree of Life represents ever greater levels of intimacy with the divine.

Christianity, Hesychasm

A completely separate contemplative movement within the Eastern Orthodox Church is Hesychasm, a form of Christian meditation. Comparisons have been made between the Hesychastic centers of prayer and the position of the chakras. Particular emphasis is placed upon the heart area. However, there is no talk about these centers as having any sort of metaphysical existence. Far more than in any of the cases discussed above, the centers are simply places to focus the concentration during prayer.

Other mystical traditions exist within Christianity. The Renaissance saw the birth of "Christian Kabbalah," which had its roots in Jewish kabala.

(end of article)

As was discussed above, the Adam creation included both a male and a female.

1. The Adam creation contained the entire ten sefirot or the Tree of Life.
2. The Adam creation duplicated the entire Tree of Life with its right and left sides, and the balance in the center.
3. Man and woman can be in total harmony only when they share a common spiritual will (Crown, the first sefira), when they agree not to destroy what is created between them (Time, or the sixth sefira), and when they agree to partake in the experience of the living universe by joining

together sexually (the ninth sefira being the astral body or the Soul) in order to produce (human bodies = children) to be occupied by these souls.

4. By fulfilling all of the above requirements, these two entities, man and woman, can become one, thereby implementing creation itself.

After creating man and woman, God gives them dominion over all his creation, according to Genesis 1:28.

Chapter 4   The Garden of Eden

Genesis 2:8 describes the Garden of Eden as a garden that was planted by God; it says he placed Adam, meaning both male and female, in the garden. Genesis 2:10 describes four rivers that originated from the Garden of Eden, including two we are familiar with: the Tigris and the Euphrates of today's Iraq (Genesis 2:14).

The third one described surrounded the entire land of Cush, in Genesis 2:13. The word *Cush* means the "black land" or the "black continent." The fourth one surrounded the entire land of Havilah, in Genesis 2:11. No one knows what the word *Havilah* means. However, we will discuss this issue later and come to understand what this land is.

After God places both the male and female Adam in the garden, he orders them to work the land and to keep it (Genesis 2:15). He also commands them not to eat from the fruit of the Tree of Knowledge of Good and Evil, in Genesis 2:16 and 17, and warns them that if they eat from it, they will die that same day. This means that as long as they do not eat from the Tree of Knowledge, they will not die and can live forever.

The location of the Tree of Knowledge and the Tree of Life is emphasized in Genesis 2:9. It says that these trees were inside the garden. But it is very clear that these trees must have been in the Garden of Eden, so why emphasize that they are inside the garden? What is meant here is that these two trees were in a garden within a garden, like an inner sanctum. God has given permission to Adam, male and female, to eat from all the trees within the Garden of Eden (Genesis 2:16), but they are forbidden to enter and eat from the inner garden where the Tree of Knowledge is (Genesis 2:17).

God warns them that if they eat from the Tree of Knowledge, they will die that same day (Genesis 2:17). Note here that God warns them not to eat from the Tree of Knowledge only, without making the same warning in regard to the Tree of Life.

Why doesn't God warn them not to eat from the Tree of Life?

The answer is very simple. The meaning of the Tree of Life becomes clear only when one has knowledge. Therefore, it is important to warn them first in regard to the Tree of Knowledge and not so important to warn them about the Tree of Life; they are living in an environment where life is eternal and eating from the Tree of Life will give them what they already have, and they will not be affected at all or know the difference, which is none.

The book of Genesis continues in chapter 2 to say that Adam was busy naming all the animals God created (Genesis 2:19–20), but that a helper for him was not found. Then the book proceeds to describe the making of a woman, whom Adam named Eve (Genesis 2:23).

We have a dilemma.

It appears that there were two creations of male and female. The first one is called Adam, in Genesis 1:26, when God says, "Let us make an Adam in our image and in our likeness, and they shall rule over the fish of the sea, and over the animals, and over the whole earth, and over every creeping thing that creeps upon the earth." In Genesis 1:27, "God creates Adam in his image, in the image of God he created him, male and female he created them."

How come, then, there is a need to create a new female, whom Adam called Eve, in Genesis 2:21–23?

Let us examine the creation of this new female.

The Bible says in Genesis 2:21–22 that Adam was put to sleep, that one rib bone was taken from his ribs, and that God took this rib and placed meat around it and created a female whom he then brought to Adam.

This description of the making of Eve seems awfully close to the process of cloning. Note that the making of Eve is not made in the presence of the male Adam, but rather somewhere else. Once Eve is completed, she is *brought* to the male Adam.

Indeed, when this female is brought to Adam, he says, in Genesis 2:23, "This time she is part of my bone and my flesh and therefore she would be called a woman." This implies that there was previously another female. It further implies that Adam was left alone for a long time until God said, "It is not good for man to be alone, let us make a helper for him" (Genesis 2:18). The creation of Eve comes after that.

Note here that as the male Adam proceeds to name Eve, he refers to her as a woman. He does not yet know what that means, because the Bible says in Genesis 2:25 that they were both naked and not ashamed with each other. This implies that they were not yet "self-aware."

However, when both Eve and the male Adam eat from the Tree of Knowledge (Genesis 3:6), they become "self-aware" and realize they are naked, and they therefore proceed to cover themselves with leaves from a fig tree, in Genesis 3:7. The male Adam calls his female clone "Eve" only after the act of acquiring knowledge, in Genesis 3:20.

When God is walking in the garden, in Genesis 3:8, they hide themselves from him within the Tree of Knowledge. This means they are self-aware and use knowledge itself to conceal themselves, knowing they have disobeyed God's command.

It is clear why they hide themselves from God, because they know they will be sentenced to death as God told them, according to Genesis 2:17. The question is, how do they hide themselves to the point where God does not know where they are?

The answer is that once they acquire infinite knowledge, they are able to hide themselves within the Tree of Knowledge itself, to the point that even God is asking, "Where are you?" This is similar to hiding a certain code of ones and zeros as in a computer binary sequence in a long sequence of ones and zeros that make up a computer program. This specific code will not be able to be detected, even by the programmer himself, unless one knows where and what to look for.

This is essentially what they do: they hide themselves within the universe of knowledge itself.

However, when God calls them and asks them about their location, in Genesis 3:9, they answer him and thereby show themselves. It is possible that they do not know that their creator doesn't know where they are. However, the excuse they use is that they are naked (Genesis 3:10) and that is why they hid themselves, not that they ate from the Tree of Knowledge and thereby disobeyed God's command. By that time, they have committed three sins: they ate from the Tree of Knowledge, they tried to conceal themselves and hide their crime because they knew they would be punished by death, and they lied to God about the reason they were hiding.

Even though God told both the male Adam and Eve that they would die if they ate from the Tree of Knowledge, in Genesis 2:17, he cannot kill them as long as they are in the Garden of Eden, where life is eternal and death does not exist.

Therefore, the only way they can die is by being banished from the interior space of the garden to the Earth environment where time, and thereby the aging process, will cause them to die.

However, there is another reason for this banishment.

Genesis 3:22 says that God said, "Behold, man has become like one of us, knowing good and evil, lest he stretch his hand and took from the Tree of Life, and ate and lived forever."

This implies that the male Adam and Eve were not yet meant to live forever, only for an undetermined period of time (as measured by us). To live forever, one must eat from the Tree of Life, and that is what God fears will happen if the male Adam and Eve are permitted to stay in the Garden of Eden, now that they have acquired infinite knowledge.

Once Adam and Eve were banished from the Garden of Eden, God placed the cherubim and the flame of the revolving sword to guard the path of the Tree of Life (Genesis 3:24).

Why did God place two separate levels of security made of the revolving sword and the cherubim to guard the entrance into Eden?

The answer is that the revolving sword was to guard against physical entry by humans, and the cherubim were there to guard against entrance into the garden with the spiritual body or, if you wish, the soul.

God wanted to ensure that humans did not have entry into the garden even if they figured out a way, either physical or spiritual, to enter into Eden.

So how does one enter into the Garden of Eden and be in the presence of God?

The answer is that only those with a pure heart may enter.

It is clear that God did not want either Adam or Eve to acquire an everlasting life, which is why he banished them from the Garden of Eden, lest they destroy heaven.

Why did God not want either Adam or Eve to acquire knowledge? And why was the punishment for acquiring such knowledge death? This seems like an extremely harsh punishment.

The answer may be that the Tree of Knowledge contained infinite knowledge of good and infinite knowledge of bad or evil, and that these new Earth creations of Adam and Eve could not handle infinite knowledge in that stage of their development. Another way of saying it is that too much knowledge in the hand of a person who does not know how to use it is dangerous and can cause great harm to all.

The question that must be asked here is whether God intended to expose Adam and Eve to the Tree of Knowledge as they developed and matured under his supervision in the Garden of Eden.

We do not know the answer to this question, because the snake changed the development cycle of humans by introducing them to the Tree of Knowledge through temptation before they were ready, in terms of their development.

We do know, however, that God intended to keep both Adam and Eve in the Garden of Eden for a purpose. It is not written anywhere that God intended to banish his creation from the garden.

Indeed, God's decision to banish Adam and Eve from the Garden of Eden becomes clear in chapter 4 of the book of Genesis.

Before proceeding to chapter 4, we want to examine the question of what happened to the first woman who was created as the female Adam together with the male Adam.

Tradition tells us (Rabbi Issac ben Jacob ha-Cohen who lived in the thirteenth century wrote on this subject. His treatise was entitled "A Treatise on the Left Emanation," the Alpha Betha of Ben Sira, and the Zohar, the book of Genesis, passages 98-102), that the female Adam (now called Lilith) joined the angel Samael shortly after they were created, which led to the creation of Eve as a clone from the male Adam to be the second female for the male Adam. The angel Samael, or as we now call him, Satan, was one of the evolved beings, or angels if you wish, who introduced the clone woman, Eve, through temptation, to the Tree of Knowledge.

Samael was careful not to expose the first woman, Lilith, or the female Adam to the Tree of Knowledge, knowing she would have the same fate as Eve, meaning eventual death. Indeed, he did not need her to acquire knowledge because she joined him willingly and fulfilled any of his commands. He tempted the second female Eve only after she was created for the male Adam, realizing that humans will be propagated by God and that the only way to stop their propagation is to kill them through the introduction to the Tree of Knowledge, which will lead to their death as promised by God. His plan was simple and deadly.

Indeed, both humans, Adam the male and Eve the female clone, did die, and Lilith still survived.

Having access to the female Adam (Lilith) within the Garden of Eden turned out to be very useful. Samael had a spy inside the Garden of Eden in the form of the female Adam, who took instruction from him without any disobedience.

Because Lilith was not exposed to the Tree of Knowledge, she was left in a state without self-awareness, and therefore could be manipulated by Samael. He used her sexuality, which could not be refused, to tempt various righteous men throughout history. However, Samael did not count on the fact that he, too, would be banished from the Garden of Eden. He regarded himself as an evolved being, and he was, thereby not considering for a moment the possibility that he himself could be punished as well. This consideration arose from the fact that he did not eat from the Tree of Knowledge (there was no need for it since he was exposed to it already), and that he only told the truth to Eve about the effect of eating from the Tree of Knowledge—that they would be like God himself, knowing good and evil, as indeed God himself said in Genesis 3:22.

This female Adam has many names and appears in various instances in the Bible and in human history, typically in a position of power where she can alter historic events. Here are some examples:

She appears in the ancient world as Ashtoreth, the Babylonian goddess alongside Baal, whom the Bible considers Satan. She appears as Potifar's wife to kill and eliminate Joseph and therefore all his seed and the future Messiah by saying that he raped her, which obviously would bring him the death sentence from his master, the minister of Pharaoh, or so she planned.

She appears as the Egyptian goddess Wadjyt during Moses's time, protecting the pharaohs, and was elevated to such a high degree that they placed her on top of their crowns.

She appears as Delilah with Samson and causes Samson to join her and thereby lose his eyesight as punishment by the forces of light; because he has joined darkness, he has lost the ability to see God's light. Note that they do not take his life, only his eyesight by which he can see light.

She later appears as Jezebel, wife of King Ahab and queen of the ten tribes of Israel. Only Elijah can defeat her, which is the reason for him being there. I will cover this story in another book. Note that Megiddo was her place of worship and that she had four hundred priests, which I will discuss later in this book. Megiddo is the site of Armageddon.

Tradition tells us that she has many other names:

- Lilith

- The holy prostitute

- Isis

- Ishtar

- Ashtoreth

- Jezebel

- Parvati (Shiva's wife) in Hindu tradition

- and many others

Chapter 5   Banishment from the Garden of Eden

As I said earlier, God could not trust having humans within the Garden of Eden any longer because of their immaturity and their exposure to infinite knowledge (Genesis 3:22). One of the first acts of the offspring of Adam and Eve was for Cain to kill Abel, which is a demonstration of what happens when infinite knowledge of good and evil is given to humans who cannot handle it yet; therefore, there was the need for immediate banishment from the Garden of Eden.

The lesson here is clear: with great knowledge or power comes great responsibility for using it. That is why God did not want Adam or Eve to live any longer within the Garden of Eden. They had great knowledge but could not always be trusted to use it correctly.

Adam and Eve are banished from the Garden of Eden by its eastern gate (this will become clear soon), which is where they settle, according to Genesis 3:24, not knowing where else to go. Before God banishes them from the garden, he makes them garments of skin (Genesis 3:21), so that they can survive in the environment of Earth for at least one of his days, which is equal to a thousand years of ours. This garment is our own skin, which covers our bodies.

Why does God banish Adam and Eve through the eastern gate? Why is it important? And how can one re-enter the Garden of Eden? Remember that God placed the flame of the revolving sword and the cherubim to guard the path to the Tree of Life in Genesis 3:24.

5.1 The spiritual chariot, or *merkavah*

The answers to these questions can be found in the book of creation, *Sefer Yetzirah,* attributed to Abraham. Rabbi Aryeh Kaplan's wonderful insight into this book is titled *Sefer Yetzirah: The Book of Creation,* published in 1990.

Sefer Yetzirah 2:4 tells us we must build a vehicle, or *merkavah,* that encapsulates the one attempting to enter the domain of the Garden of Eden. This vehicle must be made out of the twenty-two Hebrew letters, which must be constructed in one's mind from the Earth itself. The letters must be curved out from the Earth and made to stand up in a circle around the initiate. They must appear as three-dimensional structures. The head of each letter must connect with every other letter to form 231 beams, or gates, according to *Sefer Yetzirah* 2:5. This must be duplicated both above the initiate's head as a ceiling and below him as a floor. The resulting structure is an enclosure that looks like a cylinder with a flat top and bottom, as shown below.

The cylinder below shows a beam between א and ל, and between א and ט, as an example of the construction of these beams.

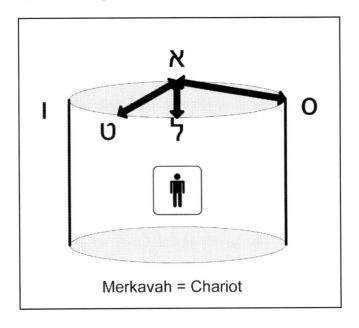

Merkavah = Chariot

The twenty-two Hebrew letters are shown below (from Wikipedia).

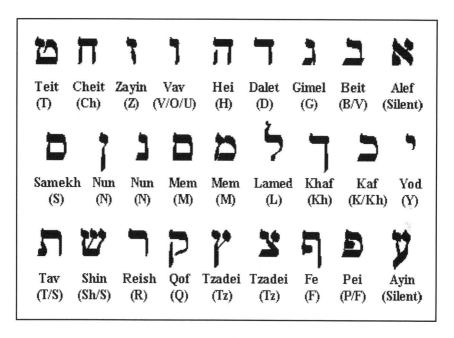

Note that Hebrew letters have numerical weights. *Aleph* through *teit* equal one through nine respectively, while *yod* through *tzadei* = ten through ninety repectively, and *qof* through *tav* = one hundred through four hundred respectively.

Once the structure of the vehicle is finished, it must be held firmly in the mind of the initiate at all times, no matter what disturbances might be ahead. Losing focus for an instant as the initiate attempts to pass through the three perils discussed below will cause immediate death.

These perils are meant to block any attempt at entrance into the garden by anyone who does not have a pure heart. This means that *only* those with purity of heart, who will never consider the destruction of heaven, will be allowed entrance. One of Jesus's teachings hints at this condition, in Matthew 5:8: "Blessed are the pure in heart, for they will see God."

What are these perils?

The prophet Ezekiel points them out in Ezekiel 1:4.

1. A great wind—today we call it a hurricane, like a category 5 or higher. The purpose is clear: to make the one entering the fifth dimension (the fifth dimension is the first spiritual dimension beyond Time, which is the fourth dimension) completely disoriented so that he will not know how to exit, perishing in the process.

2. The second peril is great fog. The purpose here again is clear: it is meant to confuse and disorient anyone trying to enter into the fifth dimension. The result of such disorientation is death to the physical body, for no exit will be located.

3. The third peril is great fire. Here again is a test of disorientation and endurance. To escape the fire of tremendous heat, one needs to shield the astral body with material that is immensely capable of withstanding heat.

The vehicle that is constructed is not made of any materials from this Earth. It must be made of the light of God, the same light that ignited the one. In other words, it must be made of Spiritual Light (the fifth through ninth dimensions) and must be navigated by Will (the tenth dimension).

The ancient ones called it a chariot. Indeed, we find that the prophet Elijah is taken into the fifth dimension by a "chariot of fire" as described by his disciple, the prophet Elisha, in the Old Testament, in 2 Kings 2:11.

We were banished from the Garden of Eden by its eastern gate, and God placed the cherubim and the revolving sword to guard the path of the Tree of Life from the east of Eden, as was stated earlier.

Let us see why that is so.

Note that the wall of the circler chariot is made of twenty-two Hebrew letters starting with *aleph,* א. If one travels exactly halfway around the circle, or eleven letters, he will arrive at *lamed,* ל. If he continues another eleven letters, he will arrive at *aleph* again. *Aleph* is therefore the origin.

Note that the path from *aleph* to *lamed* spells *EL,* which in Hebrew, לא, means "God." However, the path from *lamed* to *aleph* spells *LO,* and in Hebrew, לא, means "no."

The meaning is very clear. The path from *aleph* to *lamed* is the path to God. However, the path from *lamed* to *aleph* means that the entrance through this gate is forbidden. This is the eastern gate that God has forbidden mankind to enter. It is therefore clear that the entrance is through the path from *lamed* to *aleph* and the initiate must use *aleph* as his guiding compass. *Aleph* is the origin. The initiate must not lose sight of *aleph* at any time; otherwise he will be lost. By facing east while inside the chariot, the initiate must appeal to God, who is in *aleph.* Only if his appeal is accepted is he allowed to enter halfway through the circle, through *lamed,* which is the eastern gate.

Even if his appeal is accepted, he must be examined by the cherubim, who will determine his purity of heart. Because the entrance into the fifth dimension is through *lamed* and ending at *aleph,* we need to know more about *aleph.*

1. *Aleph* is the first letter of the Hebrew alphabet..
2. Its numerical weight is one (the Hebrew alphabet has numerical values attached to its letters).
3. It has two heads and two legs.
4. It is made of three letters: *yod, vav,* and inverse *yod.*
5. These three letters have a numerical weight of twenty-six, the same as the name of God, *yod, hei, vav, hei,* יהוה.
6. The two *yods* are separated from each other by the letter *vav,* which has a numerical value of six. These are the six days of creation.
7. The two *yods* are opposite of each other. Each has a numerical value of ten. These are the ten sefirot and their opposites.

Here we see that the ten sefirot in the first *yod* were separated from their opposite ten sefirot by the *vav,* or the six. This means that the ten sefirot that created the universe have also their opposites, and therefore a parallel universe to ours exists that is opposite in all aspects. A short discussion on this subject is given below.

5.2 Location of the Garden of Eden

As we saw from the above discussion, entrance into the garden is not that easy. But where is this Garden of Eden?

Let us try to locate it from what we know so far and from other pieces of information provided in the Bible. The landing of Noah's ark on Mount Ararat is significant and helpful in this quest.

As mentioned earlier, four rivers came out of the Garden of Eden, according to Genesis 2:10, and we named two of them. The third river is the Nile, and the fourth is an underground river that passes under the State of Israel. It starts at the southeast corner of Turkey, just above Syria and northern Iraq, and continues to the east of the Hermon mountain chain in Lebanon and into northern Israel.

Let us follow the path of this fourth river.

The first inkling we have about this river is that a fresh spring of water in the city of Safed was used by the great kabbalistic Rabbi Isaac Luria, who is also called the Ari. The Ari was the foremost rabbi Jewish mystic during the sixteenth century in the community of Safed in the Galilee region of Ottoman Palestine. He is considered the father of contemporary Kabbalah.

People have attributed healing powers to this spring from that time until now. The second mention is the spring in Nazareth, where Mary had a vision of the angel Gabriel. This spring is called Mary's well, and is the continuation of the same underground river.

The third such mention is the most important one: it is the well dug by Jezebel in Megiddo in order to reach water within the city of Magiddo. Because she was aware of this fourth river originating from Eden, she aimed to contaminate the water, which continued to Jerusalem and was used by the priests to clean and purify the vessels used in the temple of Solomon.

She contaminated this river by sacrificing humans to her mate or master, Satan (or Baal), in the city of Magiddo. This is why Elijah was sent to stop her.

These three mentions make up only one set of data. Let us examine some others.

We know that God banished Adam from the Garden of Eden and that Adam settled to its east. We also know that mankind spread from that point to occupy Mesopotamia, which is the land between southeast Turkey and the Persian Gulf. We know that Noah's ark landed not far from there on Mount Ararat.

It must be that the early descendants of Adam lived in proximity to the Garden of Eden. The flood, as was said earlier, lifted the ark and deposited it not far from that area.

What we call the devil, or the one that was banished from the Garden of Eden with Adam and Eve, has established his spiritual kingdom of evil immediately after banishment among these early descendants of Adam, who lived in proximity to the Garden of Eden.

To this day, the Yazidi of northern Syria and southeast Turkey who are just next to the Garden of Eden, worship Satan as their god. It seems that all of the above instances point to the location of the Garden of Eden being in southeast Turkey.

(start of article from Wikipedia)

Archaeological excavations and surveys carried out in and around the city of Van (Turkey) indicate that the history of human settlement in this region goes back at least as far as 5000 BC. The Tilkitepe Mound, which is on the shores of Lake Van and a few kilometers to the south of Van Castle, is the only source of information about the oldest culture of Van.

(end of article)

5.3   The age of the children of Adam and Eve

We often wonder why the children of Adam and Eve lived for hundreds of years whereas the vast majority of us today live less than one hundred years. We mistakenly assume that they did not know what a year was, and how many months in a year, and how many days in a month. However, it is clear from the book of Genesis that a clear citation was given of the number of days in a month, the number of months in the year (Genesis 7:11), and how many years a person lived. The citation also clearly shows that an exact age where a specific event took place, such as marriage or the delivery of a child, is registered.

The question is, why did these earlier generations live for such a long time?

The answer is that the Earth needed to be populated and that therefore the earlier generations needed to live longer to make many children. Indeed, Adam himself continued to have many more children beyond Cain, Abel, and Seth, according to Genesis 5:4. However, as mankind increased in number, God decided to reduce the age of man to 120 years (Genesis 6:3).

How was this done? We know from science that our cells decay because of environmental damage. This damage can be caused by various things, such as cosmic radiation, sunrays, weather, exposure to various chemicals, and so on.

If there is no regeneration of the cells to what they were at birth, the cells keep decaying, losing their original identity, and we simply age and die.

To have long life, one must have constant cell regeneration, as if the cells have not divided yet or are original cells. Today, we are searching for this fountain of youth through stem cells. We are hoping to be able to reprogram stem cells so that we can regenerate cells as they were at their original state. Furthermore, we may be able to program them to be different cells of various kinds that can be grown into various organs, as we wish.

Some research has already taken place where cells are injected into damaged heart tissues to help them regenerate. There is some success in this area, as shown below.

Moshe Mazin

Stem Cell information

(start of article from The National Institutes of Health, U.S. Department of Health and Human Services, 2009

Heart attacks and congestive heart failure remain among the Nation's most prominent health challenges despite many breakthroughs in cardiovascular medicine. In fact, despite successful approaches to prevent or limit cardiovascular disease, the restoration of function to the damaged heart remains a formidable challenge. Recent research is providing early evidence that adult and embryonic stem cells may be able to replace damaged heart muscle cells and establish new blood vessels to supply them. Discussed here are some of the recent discoveries that feature stem cell replacement and muscle regeneration strategies for repairing the damaged heart.

Recently, Orlic and colleagues reported on an experimental application of hematopoietic stem cells for the regeneration of the tissues in the heart. In this study, a heart attack was induced in mice by tying off a major blood vessel, the left main coronary artery. Through the identification of unique cellular surface markers, the investigators then isolated a select group of adult primitive bone marrow cells with a high capacity to develop into cells of multiple types. When injected into the damaged wall of the ventricle, these cells led to the formation of new cardiomyocytes, vascular endothelium, and smooth muscle cells, thus generating de novo myocardium, including coronary arteries, arterioles, and capillaries. The newly formed myocardium occupied 68 percent of the damaged portion of the ventricle nine days after the bone marrow cells were transplanted, in effect replacing the dead myocardium with living, functioning tissue. The researchers found that mice that received the transplanted cells survived in greater numbers than mice with heart attacks that did not receive the mouse stem cells.

Follow-up experiments are now being conducted to extend the post transplantation analysis time to determine the longer-range effects of such therapy. The partial repair of the damaged heart muscle suggests that the transplanted mouse hematopoietic stem cells responded to signals in the environment near the injured myocardium. The cells migrated to the damaged region of the ventricle, where they multiplied and became "specialized" cells that appeared to be cardiomyocytes.

(end of article)

Is it possible that early man, from Adam to Noah, had a cell regeneration mechanism?

If so, how did it work?

It seems that the answer to this question was just published in the journal *Nature*, on November 28, 2010.

A team of research scientists led by Dr. Ronald DePinho from Harvard Medical School was able to reverse the aging process in elderly mice. The Harvard team focused on the telomere shortening process, which is a protective cap at the end of each of our twenty-three pairs of chromosomes that carry our DNA. When the cell divides, this protective cap is shortened until it eventually does not allow any more cell division. Aging is a direct result of this process. The team showed that by using an enzyme called telomerase, they were able to stop the telomere caps from getting shorter and caused the aging process to stop and even to regenerate damaged tissues all over the body, including the brain.

Let us now return to the question posed earlier about the age of Adam and his descendants.

The answer to this question is the solution to a very long life and possibly to immortality.

Let us examine this issue in more detail.

We know that God has caused mankind's age to decrease from about 950–960 to 120, and achieving 120 is difficult. To do this, there must exists a mechanism within us that can be programmed by God or these advance beings to increase or decrease our cell regeneration mechanism (as we just witnessed with the Harvard cell regeneration breakthrough).

A direct proof of this mechanism of lengthening or shortening the length of life in humans is given in Isaiah 38:4–8, where God grants King Hezekiah fifteen additional years. This can easily be done through the use of telomerase enzyme, as discussed above.

Because no direct physical contact with God or these advanced beings is reported anywhere in human history other than the creation of Adam and the clone woman, Eve, one must conclude that such programming is done to us externally by remote means.

If that is the case, there must be within us a controller/processor/receiver that can respond to remote commands and process them.

Such a controller or processor (computer) must be embedded within our brain, because it is the most logical location to place it (we can exist without limbs, but we can't exist without a head).

Furthermore, there must be two such processors, one in the right lobe and one in the left lobe of our brain. These controllers must be molecularly based organic processors. This kind of technology is not out of the realm of possibility. In fact, some current research is investigating such processors, as shown below.

Molecular processors

(start of article from Wikipedia)

Molecular processors are currently in their infancy and currently only a few exist. At present a basic molecular processor is any biological or chemical system that uses a complementary DNA (cDNA) template to form a long chain amino acid molecule. A key factor that differentiates molecular processors is "the ability to control output" of protein or peptide concentration as a function of time. Simple formation of a molecule becomes the task of a chemical reaction, bioreactor or other polymerization technology. Current molecular processors take advantage of cellular processes to produce amino acid–based proteins and peptides. The formation of a molecular processor currently involves integrating cDNA into the genome and should not replicate and re-insert, or be defined as a virus after insertion. Current molecular processors are replication incompetent, non-communicable and cannot be transmitted from cell to cell, animal to animal or human to human. All must have a method to terminate if implanted. The most effective methodology for insertion of cDNA (template with control mechanism) uses capsid technology to insert a payload into the genome. A viable molecular processor is one that dominates cellular function by re-task and or re-assignment but does not terminate the cell. It will continuously produce protein or produce on demand and have method to regulate dosage if qualifying as a "drug delivery" molecular processor. Potential applications range from up-regulation of functional CFTR in Cystic Fibrosis and Hemoglobin in Sickle Cell Anemia to angiogenesis in cardiovascular stenosis to account for protein deficiency (used in gene therapy.)

(end of article)

Chapter 6   The Generation of Noah

The most likely location for such processors is the thalamus, which is within our brain. By relaying remote commands to these processors, one can control the rate of cell regeneration and their quality (like photocopies of a photograph that become less and less clear, caused by loss of the information that appeared in the original photograph).

Recently, a group of researchers from Japan and Michigan Technological University (*Nature Physics* 2010) were able to demonstrate a working molecular processor which can solve complex problems that currently use supercomputers. The molecular processor acts much like our brain to perform massive parallel computing to solve complex problems, whereas conventional supercomputers perform computation in serial mode, which typically is much slower.

This indeed could have been the mechanism by which the age of humans was controlled. If that is the case, then many of the statements in the Bible that say, "God spoke to …" become possible and credible, since there was direct transmission of specific commands into these processors in the brain. When the Bible says God spoke to Noah or Abraham or anyone else, it is now clear how this was done.

We now may be able to understand the significance of the Tree of Life. The Tree of Life contains the program or the commands that enable continuous regeneration of our cells in their original form, thereby making us immortal.

Because Cain has killed his brother Abel, God does not choose any of his descendants to be a potential conduit between him and humans. God waits until Adam has another child, by the name of Seth, in Genesis 4:25. Adam is 130 years old when he has Seth.

Enoch, who was five generations from Seth, according to Genesis 5:3–20, is the one God chooses to be with for three hundred years while he is flesh and blood. He then takes him from among his family and is no longer on Earth (Genesis 5:24).

The Jewish Kabbala tells us that Enoch became the top angel, known as Matatron, and that he was one of the two angels of the Holy Spirit on top of the ark of the covenant.

In chapter 6 of Genesis it says that as the children of man multiplied on Earth, "the children of God saw that the daughters of men were good-looking and they took them as mates from whomever they chose" (Genesis 6:2).

Out of this union came the Nephilim, according to Genesis 6:4. This union between the children of God and the daughters of men was not what God wanted. He saw that only evil could come out of this union, in Genesis 6:3, and decided to end all life on Earth, in Genesis 6:7.

It is likely that the Nephilim, who were a hybrid between the children of God (these are not the children of Adam) and the daughters of men, abused their power or suffocated the development of mankind, since these humans were inferior to them in intellect and can be abused easily.

However, he found Noah, a direct descendant of Adam and Eve, to be a righteous man, and decided to continue humanity's existence through him.

We now have a question. What is meant by "the children of God"?

Many opinions and interpretations are given to this passage. However, it is clear that "the book of Genesis" means literally the "children of God." Furthermore, it is made clear in Genesis that the children of God took the daughters of men as mates. This union could be possible only if the children of God were flesh and blood. We must ask how it is possible for the children of God to be flesh and blood.

Is it possible that the children of God were just evolved beings?

After all, humans were made in their image and in their likeness, according to Genesis 1:26. The only difference between humans and the children of God is that humans became flesh and blood after they were banished from the Garden of Eden, and God made them clothing of skin, meaning our natural skin, in order to survive on Earth, whereas the children of God were not banished to Earth's environment. Is it possible that the children of God could choose to be on Earth by will? And, in doing so, they can become flesh and blood?

This passage in the Bible is difficult, because it reminds us of Greek mythology and the many acts that the gods of Olympus did with humans, both male and female.

However, is it out of the realm of possibility that evolved beings could transform into a state of flesh and blood?

Let us examine this concept in more detail.

We know from Einstein's theory of relativity that energy is equaled to mass multiplied by the square root of the speed of light. This means that mass and energy are related to each other by the square of the speed of light, and that matter has two states of existence, particles or energy. Currently, we know how to convert mass into energy. But we do not know yet how to convert energy into mass. The question here is this: is it possible that these evolved beings knew how to convert energy into mass? If this is possible, then the idea of beings made of energy that can convert themselves into physical mass is not difficult to understand. This means that these evolved beings have very advanced technology compared with us.

Furthermore, they also must have a teleportation technology, which would allow them to move energy or mass from one point to the next at the speed of light or a multiple of it. It is not sufficient to have a technology for converting energy into mass; one also needs a teleportation technology to move from one point to the next.

It is clear that if these beings crossed over from a plane of existence that was made of energy into a physical plane of existence, they needed a teleportation technology in addition to being able to convert energy into mass or matter.

The report below, commissioned by the US government and available to the public, explains in detail the possibilities of teleportation technology. Only an abstract and preface are included here. The report is more than eighty pages of scientific materials with complex mathematical formulas. The rest of it can be found online.

(start of article from office of management and budget OMB No. 0704-0188)

REPORT DOCUMENTATION PAGE *Form Approved*

OMB No. 0704-0188

14. ABSTRACT

This study was tasked with the purpose of collecting information describing the teleportation of material objects, providing a description of teleportation as it occurs in physics, its theoretical and experimental status, and a projection of potential applications. The study also consisted of a search for teleportation phenomena occurring naturally or under laboratory conditions that can be assembled into a model describing the conditions required to accomplish the transfer of objects. This included a review and documentation of quantum teleportation, its theoretical basis, technological development, and its potential applications. The characteristics of teleportation were defined and physical theories were evaluated in terms of their ability to completely describe the phenomena. Contemporary physics, as well as theories that presently challenge the current physics paradigm were investigated. The author identified and proposed two unique physics models for teleportation that are based on the manipulation of either the general relativistic space-time metric or the space-time vacuum electromagnetic (zero-point fluctuations) parameters. Naturally occurring anomalous teleportation phenomena that were previously studied by the United States and foreign governments were also documented in the study and are reviewed in the report. The author proposes an additional model for teleportation that is based on a combination of the experimental results from the previous government studies and advanced physics concepts. Numerous recommendations outlining proposals for further theoretical and experimental studies are given in the report. The report also includes an extensive teleportation bibliography.

Preface

The Teleportation Physics Study is divided into four phases. Phase I is a review and documentation of quantum teleportation, its theoretical basis, technological development, and its potential application.

Phase II developed a textbook description of teleportation as it occurs in classical physics, explored its theoretical and experimental status, and projected its potential applications. Phase III consisted of a search for teleportation phenomena occurring naturally or under laboratory conditions that can be assembled into a model describing the conditions required to accomplish the disembodied conveyance of objects. The characteristics of teleportation were defined, and physical theories were evaluated in terms of their ability to completely describe the phenomenon. Presently accepted physics theories, as well as theories that challenge the current physics paradigm were investigated for completeness. The theories that provide the best chance of explaining teleportation were selected, and experiments with a high chance of accomplishing teleportation were identified. Phase IV is the final report.

The report contains five chapters. Chapter 1 is an overview of the textbook descriptions for the various teleportation phenomena that are found in nature, in theoretical physics concepts, and in experimental laboratory work. Chapter 2 proposes two quasi-classical physics concepts for teleportation: the first is based on engineering the space-time metric to induce a traversable wormhole; the second is based on the polarizable-vacuum-general relativity approach that treats space-time metric changes in terms of equivalent changes in the vacuum permittivity and permeability constants. These concepts are theoretically developed and presented. Promising laboratory experiments were identified and recommended for further research. Chapter 3 presents the current state-of-art of quantum teleportation physics, its theoretical basis, technological development, and its applications. Key theoretical, experimental, and applications breakthroughs were identified, and a series of theoretical and experimental research programs are proposed to solve technical problems and advance quantum teleportation physics.

Chapter 4 gives an overview of alternative teleportation concepts that challenge the present physics paradigm. These concepts are based on the existence of parallel universes/spaces and/or extra space dimensions. The theoretical and experimental work that has been done to develop these concepts is reviewed, and a recommendation for further research is made. Last, Chapter 5 gives an in-depth overview of unusual teleportation phenomena that occur naturally and under laboratory conditions. The teleportation phenomenon discussed in the chapter is based on psychokinesis (PK), which is a category of psychotronics. The U.S. military-intelligence literature is reviewed, which relates the historical scientific research performed on PK-teleportation in the U.S., China and the former Soviet Union. The material discussed in the chapter largely challenges the current physics paradigm; however, extensive controlled and repeatable laboratory data exists to suggest that PK-teleportation is quite real and that it is controllable. The report ends with a combined list of references.

(end of article)

As one can see from the above study, teleportation technology is a possibility. As an additional note, the cohabitation of the evolved beings and humans might explain the various gigantic structures around the Earth such as pyramids and the Sphinx. A teleportation technology was available at that time and can explain the lifting of massive rocks into an exact position hundreds of feet above ground.

6.1 Noah and the flood

The story of Noah is well known, as told in Genesis 6, 7, and 8. However, the main point that I want to make here is that Noah's ark came to rest on dry ground on the seventeenth day of the seventh month on the mountain of Ararat, according to Genesis 8:4. As I said before, the count of the days in a month and the number of months in a year was very clear. Additionally, the Bible tells us that the water covered the peaks of the highest mountains to a level of fifteen feet above them (Genesis 7:20), and the water continued to rise for 150 days (Genesis 7:24). This could happen only if the ice that covered all of Europe and North America melted away. That implies that Noah's time was around the end of the last ice age, which, according to science, happened about twelve thousand years ago, as suggested by the article below. Why did no one of Noah's generation survive?

After all, they had advanced technology sufficient enough to build ships. It must be that the melting of the glaciers over Europe, North

America, and possibly other places happened over a period of time that was too short to allow the construction of large ships. What God told Noah was simply to build a box large enough to house his entire family and many of the animals of the Earth. Noah's ark did not have any propulsion mechanism, or sails, or any other means of steering itself; it was simply a box meant to hold living creatures until the flooding that covered the entire ancient world receded.

It is clear that if the glaciers were heated over a short period of time, they would produce an enormous steam vapor that would climb up into the atmosphere and be cooled down by the height, carried over the jet stream, and deposited as constant heavy rain over the ancient world.

A discussion of this mechanism follows.

(start of article from Wikipedia)

Air and water vapor density interactions at equal temperatures

At the same temperature, a column of dry air will be denser or heavier than a column of air containing any water vapor. Thus, any volume of dry air will sink if placed in a larger volume of moist air. Also, a volume of moist air will rise or be buoyant if placed in a larger region of dry air. As the temperature rises the proportion of water vapor in the air increases, and its buoyancy will increase. The increase in buoyancy can have a significant atmospheric impact, giving rise to powerful, moisture rich, upward air currents when the air temperature and sea temperature reaches 25°C or above. This phenomenon provides a significant motivating force for cyclonic and anticyclone weather systems (tornadoes and hurricanes).

(end of article)

Constant rain could certainly have caused the entire ancient world to be flooded, possibly under several hundred feet of water or more.

Because Noah was not far from southeast Turkey, on the northwest corner of Mesopotamia, his ark was simply carried by the flood and floated, at most, several hundred miles from its original location. It landed on Mount Ararat, which is not far from the corner of southeast Turkey. Note that there was no tsunami that could destroy Noah's ark, but simply constant heavy rain and flooding. The Bible mentions that there were waves (Genesis 8:3) and that they settled down to a neutral state (Genesis 8:5). It says these waves moved from one side to the other like tides that hit a barrier and bounced back. This cyclical wave action or tides, helped keep Noah's ark at a very short distance from its original location, which by my estimate is near the southeast corner of today's Turkey as discussed in chapter 5.2 above.

The story of Noah implies that the Earth went through a rapid increase in temperature, which definitely could cause major flooding over a significant portion of the planet. Because Noah was told to build the ark, which was a box, as I said earlier, he was prepared for the flood and therefore survived. The other people who lived with him in the ancient world did not have sufficient time to build anything, and they all drowned.

Note that God instructs Noah to build a simple ark just to house himself, his family, and the animals. Its simple structure as a box was not meant to attract attention from the people living in proximity to him. The task given to Noah was sufficient to be done by him, his children, and possibly some helpers, but it certainly did not attract attention for being a high-technology structure. It could easily have passed as simply a large house. They understood the purpose of the ark only after Noah sealed himself, his family, and all the animals inside, just before the rain started. Once the rain started, it was very heavy and very fast, and none of the other people could build anything under those conditions.

It appears that the heating of the glaciers was done on purpose and not as a natural phenomenon of planetary interaction.

Once the floodwaters settled into today's seas and lakes, we find out, the Sea of Galilee, the Dead Sea, and the Great Bitter Lake of Egypt, which is between Egypt and the Sinai, were created. Many other water reservoirs were created, but our main interest is these three bodies of water.

An important point must be made in regard to the story of Noah: after Noah leaves the ark, he sacrifices several pure or clean animals to God as thanks for saving him and his family from destruction. Only after the aroma of the sacrifice that Noah has made reaches God, and only after God smells this aroma, does he decide not to destroy humanity again. The issue of the sacrifice and the smell of the aroma will be dealt with later in the book of Exodus, which is currently being written.

Chapter 7 The Seventy Nations of the Earth

In Genesis 9:1, God blesses Noah and his children and says to them, "Be fruitful and multiply and fill the earth." He then makes a covenant with Noah and his sons that he will never again destroy the Earth (Genesis 9:11).

The tenth chapter of Genesis lists the exact number of descendants who have been created from Noah: seventy. These seventy descendants created the seventy nations that have spread over the ancient world and Mesopotamia, used one language, and had common purpose (Genesis 11:1). It seems that this is exactly what people on Earth are trying to achieve at this time. Note that if one counts Noah and his wife, the number becomes seventy-two.

Several passages in the Bible deal with the numbers seventy and seventy-two. We come across the first mention when the house of Jacob enters Egypt as a household numbering seventy people, in Genesis 46:27.

The second encounter in the Bible of the number seventy-two is in Exodus 14:19–21. In each of the three sentences, the number of letters is exactly seventy-two. The third encounter with this number is the seventy elders of Israel (Genesis 24:1). If we include Moses and Aaron, the number becomes seventy-two again.

In the Zohar, and in the book of light, the Bahir, which can be dated to the first century and possibly earlier, the number seventy-two has extreme importance. If one combines the letters in the three sentences mentioned above in the correct order, one can find one of the names for God. However, the names for God are more complicated than that.

It is sufficient to mention here that the number seventy-two is indeed a special number and has special meanings. One of the names of God consists of seventy-two aspects of the divine. The fourth encounter of the number seventy is when the people of Israel are exiled to Babylon and become conquered people under the rule of the Babylonian empire for exactly seventy years as prophesied by Jeremiah (Jeremiah 25:11–12).

In some Kabbalistic books, the name of God is known as Yahweh, which in Hebrew is spelled *Yod, Hah, Vav, Hah*, (יהוה י). When arranged as a pyramid it yields the number seventy-two. The pyramid that is on the dollar bill was derived from this knowledge.

7.1 The Tower of Babel

This story of the Tower of Babel and the confusion that spread among the people who were building the city and the tower is well known, from Genesis 11:1–9. However, there appears to be one point that is difficult to understand: why would God come down from heaven to spread confusion among the people who wanted to build a city and a tower within it (Genesis 11:7)?

After all, the knowledge required to build a city and a high-rise tower within it shows that these people possessed advanced technology. A tower in excess of a hundred floors would certainly collapse if they did not possess the technology needed to build it properly. Even today, such an endeavor is very difficult to achieve. Indeed, this passage shows us that these people possessed advanced technology that they shared with all the people of the ancient world through the use of one language.

Furthermore, the Bible says that these people had a common language and common purpose (Genesis 11:6), which would be extremely useful in today's world. They are necessary if the people of Earth try to undertake major projects that would benefit mankind as a whole, such as cleaning the atmosphere of toxic gases or providing food for everyone.

Why then did God spread confusion among the people at that time (Genesis 11:7)?

The answer to this dilemma is explained below.

The description in Genesis of the settlement of the people at that time indicates that they settled as far south as the Persian Gulf and as far north as the mountains of Turkey, as far west as Lebanon and south to the Red Sea. This means that they basically settled in the Middle East. By their own testimony, in Genesis 11:4, they did not want to be spread all over the Earth, because at that time it may have appeared to them to be infinite in size; therefore they did not want to be disconnected from one another. To this end, they proposed to build a capital city that would serve to house many of their people in a central location (Genesis 11:4), much as we do today.

However, God did not want the children of Adam to be concentrated only in the Middle East; rather he wanted them spread across the entire world. This appears to be the reason for dividing the people into many languages: so they could seek different areas to live in that accommodate specific groups with the same language and possibly with the same culture. In addition to the dilemma stated above, we must note that after this spread of the people from Babylon, the age of the average person decreases substantially. The age drops to around two hundred years versus the seven hundred, eight hundred, and nine hundred years that the people of Noah's time used to live. We must remember that God has limited the age of man to around 120 years (Genesis 6:3) and that this was done gradually over some period of time, possibly by genetic engineering, as discussed earlier. We see evidence of this through the age of Terah, the father of Abraham, who lived to be 205 years old, whereas Abraham lived to be 175 years old, Isaac lived to 180, and Jacob lived to 147. Those who came after them lived shorter lives.

Chapter 8   Abraham is Chosen by God

The story of Abraham starts when his father, Terah, decides to leave Ur Kasdim (Genesis 11:31), which is in the south of today's Iraq, in the land of the Chaldeans, and moves to Haran in the north. The people of Ur practiced all kinds of pagan worship; the major deities among them were Inanna or Ishtar (Ashtoreth in the Bible), and Marduk or Baal in the Bible (www.crystalinks.com/sumergods.html).

At the same time, in Canaan, just west of the Chaldean kingdom, the people of Canaan also worshipped Baal and Ashtoreth. In short, these deities were well-established gods in the ancient world.

Why did these people worship Baal and Ashtoreth, deities the Bible portrayed as evil?

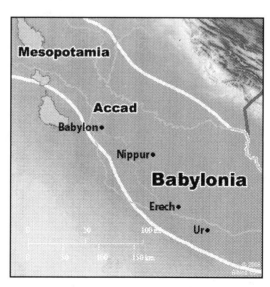

To answer this question let us look again at the Garden of Eden. Chapter 2 of Genesis has a description of the source of water that irrigates the Garden of Eden. It is said that this source split into four rivers, two of which are the Tigris and Euphrates in today's Iraq. The third river is the Nile in Egypt, and the fourth is an underground river originating in southeast Turkey and passing under the State of Israel.

As discussed earlier, the ancient world was made up of the land between the Persian Gulf, upper Iraq, southeast Turkey, and south to Egypt. However, the region between southeast Turkey and the Persian Gulf, known as Mesopotamia, was home to the original settlement of mankind.

When Noah's ark landed on Mount Ararat and the people came onto dry land, they proceeded to settle the entire region mentioned above.

As mentioned in the Bible, the snake, an evolved being who talked Eve into acquiring knowledge from the Tree of Knowledge before she and Adam were ready to accept responsibility for it, was also banished from among the other evolved beings who were in the Garden of Eden to the Earth environment outside the Graden of Eden, in Genesis 3:14–15. It is not at all surprising that this evolved being influenced the humans at that time to accept him as God, and in his anger against the other evolved beings who banished him from among them, decided to corrupt the minds of all humans whom they created—a sort of retribution, if you wish.

The Bible says in Genesis 12:1 that God tells Abraham to leave the city of Haran and go to a land that he will show him.

Abraham is seventy-five years old at that time, and Sarah, his wife, is sixty-five (Genesis 12:4). They travel to Canaan and stop near Shechem (today's Nablus), at a place called Beth El, which means the "house of God" (Genesis 12:6 and 8).

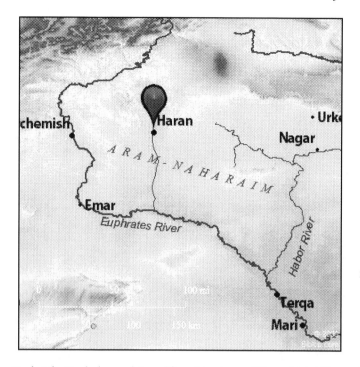

At Beth El, God shows himself to Abraham (Genesis 12:7), and tells him he will give this land to his descendants, after which Abraham builds an altar to God. However, Abraham does not stay there. He moves his tent to the top of the mountain east of Beth El, which makes Beth El to his west or toward the Mediterranean Sea, and a place called Ai to his east (Genesis 12:8). He builds another altar there and calls in the name of God.

The Bible does not say that God shows himself to Abraham at this second site, where he builds a second altar, only that Abraham calls in the name of God at that site (Genesis 12:8). This act of calling in the name of God means that Abraham has literally pronounced the actual name of God. Oral tradition refers to this name as the "uncommenteted name." No one knows the actual pronunciation of God's name, but oral tradition insists that it does exist and that by pronouncing it, one can enlist the help of God in his endeavors.

We see here that Abraham was familiar with the name of God, and he calls upon him at the second site.

Tradition tells us that these two sites are the mountain of Gerizim and the mountain of Ebal.

Located between Mt. Gerizim (left) and Mt. Ebal (right)
Shechem is preeminent in the biblical record, beginning with
God's promise of the land to Abraham.

(from BiblePlaces.com)

Why did Abraham move his tent from Mount Gerizim to Mount Ebal?

Rashi (Rabbi Shlomo Itzhaki, France, 1040–1105) interprets this act as Abraham thanking God for informing him that his descendants will inherit this land.

However, he was already told by God, in Genesis 12:2, that he would make him a great nation, and it is clear that he meant his descendants.

The reason Abraham moved his tent from one mountain to the next after seeing God is that he was very familiar with the ten dimensions of the universe, or sefirot, as was discussed earlier. He understood that when one side, the right side of the Tree of Life, Love or the Creator being the seventh sefira from the bottom, gives him a blessing, he must also invoke the name of God on the left side of the Tree of Life, which in this case is Might, or the sixth sefira from the bottom.

In this way, he balanced these forces and could achieve harmony or balance, which is the fifth sefira from the bottom, as discussed extensively earlier.

After these events, Abraham travels south to the Negev Desert.

Genesis 12:10 tells us that Abraham travels to Egypt because of widespread famine in the land. Note that Sarah is over sixty-five years old but still extremely beautiful. Indeed, Abraham is afraid the Egyptians will kill him to possess her because of her beauty (Genesis 12:12). He then tells Sarah that if she is asked about her relationship with him, she should say that he is her brother (Genesis 12:13).

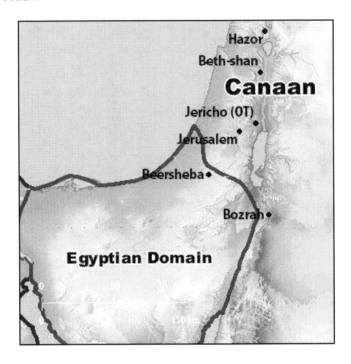

Indeed, when they reach Egypt, the Egyptians find her to be a very beautiful woman, and they take her to the house of Pharaoh (Genesis 12:15). As for Abraham, the Egyptians give him many gifts, such as slaves, both male and female, donkeys, camels, and horses on her behalf.

The question that must be asked here is this: how is it possible that Sarah is over sixty-five years old but her beauty still surpasses that of a young woman?

Let us examine this phenomenon.

Remember that Abraham is seventy-five years old when he leaves the city of Haran, which he does because God tells him to do so. This is the first instance in which God speaks to Abraham. Indeed, Abraham fulfills the command that God asks of him. In doing so, he is now under the guidance and protection of God. He and his descendants are chosen by God as a light to the nations (Genesis 12:3).

Only when he reaches Israel and comes to the plain of Moreh, and Beth El, does God appear to him. This is the first time God appears to Abraham and, in doing so, Abraham is transformed through the contact with a being of light, in the same manner that happened to Moses in the book of Exodus, although not to the same extent. Note that Moses entered into the cloud and was within it for forty days and nights, according to Exodus 24:18, which is a long period of exposure compared with the contact Abraham had.

It appears that any contact with an evolved being causes those contacted to remain young, as if time had no effect on them. We find that to be true with Moses. The Bible tells us that even though Moses was 120 years of age, he appeared to be a young man with all his faculties and physical attributes intact (Deuteronomy 34:7). It appears that Abraham had the same experience as Moses, and because of his intimate physical contact with his wife, Sarah, she too regained her youthfulness.

It is possible that the mechanism discussed earlier for the regeneration of cells occurred here for Abraham and was transferred from him to Sarah. After all, the Egyptians were not blind; they knew a young woman from an old one, and Sarah appeared to be young.

This encounter with God and the enlightenment and selection of Abraham and therefore his seed explains several other encounters later in the Bible. For example, when the slave girl Hagar is pregnant with Abraham's child and is banished to the desert, where she nearly dies from dehydration, an angel appears to provide her with water so that she and the child will not die (Genesis 21:17–19). It appears that the seed of Abraham is blessed and guarded by these evolved beings.

This means that not only the children of Israel are blessed, but also the other children of Abraham. Although God later decides that the children of Jacob are the ones who should receive his laws in the form of the Ten Commandments rather than the other children of Abraham, nevertheless, the other children of Abraham are still blessed.

We must note here that among the slaves who were given to Abraham by the pharaoh of Egypt was the slave girl Hagar. The Jewish Midrash has elevated Hagar's stature to that of a princess of Egypt; however, no such account is given in the Bible.

After the house of Pharaoh experiences several plagues while Sarah is there, the pharaoh of Egypt understands that she is Abraham's wife and not his sister (Genesis 12:17). He then decides to send her back to Abraham and to banish both of them and their household from Egypt.

It is often asked why Abraham asked Sarah to say that she was his sister and not his wife.

Let us examine this in detail.

In Genesis 11:29, it says Abraham and his brother Nahor took women as their mates. Sarah is named as Abraham's wife and Milcah as Nahor's wife. The Bible continues by saying that Milcah is the daughter of their brother Haran. There is no mention about the relationship of Sarah to Abraham. It appears that Abraham is asking Sarah to lie for him.

However, later, in Genesis 20:2, Abraham again asks Sarah to say that she is his sister in order to protect him from King Abimelech of Gerar, a city to which he has moved.

When God intervenes again on behalf of Sarah, King Abimelech discovers that Sarah is Abraham's wife and not his sister (Genesis 20:3). When he asks Abraham to clarify this, in Genesis 20:9, Abraham tells him that Sarah is his sister from the same father but not from the same mother. So indeed, Abraham was speaking the truth when he called Sarah his sister. She is his half sister.

However, many scholars, including Rashi, keep insisting that Sarah was the daughter of Haran, his younger brother who died while they were in Ur (Genesis 11:28). Rashi claims that her name was Iscah (Genesis 11:29).

We know that Sarah was ten years younger than Abraham (Genesis 17:17), and we also know that Haran was born after Abraham and Nahor (Genesis 11:27). Assuming normal pregnancy cycles of a year and a half to two years, Haran was at least three to four years younger than Abraham. Because Sarah is ten years younger than Abraham, it is simply impossible for her to have been Haran's child when he was six years old.

Therefore, the statement that Abraham makes to the pharaoh of Egypt and to King Abimelech of Gerar is correct. Sarah is his half sister.

The Bible does not tell us why God chose Abraham as a person deserving divine blessing and guidance and, later on, as worthy of receiving God's covenant.

There is no answer in the Bible to this question. However, we know from oral traditions that Abraham recognized the existence of God as the creator of all things rather than the pagan gods that were worshipped at that time.

The oral tradition supplements the written Bible and explains some of its difficult passages.

The oral traditions tell us that Abraham was able to process and understand the entire creation, (in *Sefer Yetzirah* 6:7), and to reach the conclusion that God is the only force responsible for creation itself. By doing so, he rejected all the pagan gods made from stone and other materials that were worshipped at that time. By uncovering these facts, the evolved beings, sometimes referred to as angels, recognized that Abraham was unique among the humans of Earth, and they named him and thereby his seed to be the chosen people deserving of God's guidance and laws. After all, God's laws are useful only to those who understand them; they are meaningless to those who do not.

The choice for Abraham was simple. After all, the knowledge of man's interaction with God was lost from the time of Adam (because of the flood) and was diluted after Noah by the evolved being that was banished from the Garden of Eden, namely Satan.

The word *Satan,* (ן ט ש), is derived from the Hebrew word that means "to divert," meaning to cause a person to change his path. It means that if a person was on a certain path that was righteous and good, then Satan sought to divert him into a path of wickedness, as he did with Eve.

Abraham was able to understand this entire account between man and God, and decided to follow God's guidance. For this he was rewarded as the person chosen to receive God's blessings and laws. It is implied that Abraham passed on the knowledge of creation through a series of statements that were two thousand words long and later summarized in a book, called the Book of Creation. The Book of Creation, written in Hebrew and Aramaic, is a collection of short statements with incredible impact. It is hard to understand, but its understanding leads to enlightenment. Exact knowledge of the components of this book and how it can be used is what was passed on from Abraham to Isaac to Jacob and so on. Rabbi Aryeh Kaplan discusses it in great detail in *Sefer Yetzirah* or the Book of Creation. The reader is urged to read this book for deeper understanding.

After leaving the land of Egypt behind, Abraham continues all the way back to the plain of Moreh, where God appeared to him the first time (Genesis 13:4) and where he built an altar to God. There, he calls the name of God in his prayers. Abraham recognizes that this place is holy, which is why he travels back from Egypt to the same place where God appeared to him the first time.

Indeed, later on when the people of Israel cross the Jordan River with the ark of the covenant, they build the tent of the covenant in that same spot and with the ark in it. The knowledge of the exact location where Abraham built the altar must have been passed from generation to generation all the way down to Joshua's time.

Chapter 9   Sodom and Gomorrah

Genesis 13:7 tells us that because of the great wealth of Abraham and his nephew Lot, there was strife between Abraham's shepherds and Lot's shepherds. Thereafter, Abraham suggests to Lot that they go separate ways (Genesis 13:9). Genesis 13:10 tells us that Lot chooses to go into the fertile valley of Sodom, also called the valley of Siddim. There were five cities in the valley of Siddim, which is the plain surrounding the Dead Sea of today: Sodom, Gomorrah, Adama, Zebolim, and Zoar. All these cities were conquered cities under the rule of King Chedolaomer of Elam in the north (Genesis 14:4). They remained conquered cities for twelve years, and in the thirteenth year they rebelled against King Chedolaomer for thirteen years.

Indeed, the four kings of the north are able to defeat the kings of these cities, and the kings of Sodom and Gomorrah escape and hide in the clay wells to escape death.

However, Lot is living in Sodom with his wife and daughters. They are captured and taken north into Shinar (Genesis 14:12).

When Abraham is notified that his nephew Lot has been taken by the kings of the north, he arms 318 of his men, including the three landlords who own the land he lives on, in order to chase them and to free his nephew and the people who were taken captive (Genesis 14:14–15).

Indeed, Abraham catches up with the four kings around the city of Dan in northern Israel. He uses the cover of night to raid the camp and capture or kill all of the armies of these four kings. He continues to do battle all the way to Hobah, which is west of Damascus (Genesis 14:15).

Abraham is able to free all the people who were captured and to recapture all the wealth that was taken by the four kings of the north. He then returns the people and all the goods that were taken to the five kings of the plain of Siddim without taking anything, even though the king of Sodom offers Abraham the entire wealth if he will only return the people of Sodom to him. Abraham rejects the king's offer and does not take anything in return for his deeds. He asks only that some of the people who went with him—Aner, Eshcol, and Mamre—be given their share (Genesis 14:24).

Chapter 10   God's Covenant
with Abraham

After this account in the Bible, God appears to Abraham in a vision where he promises him that his descendants will occupy the land (Genesis 15:4). When Abraham asks God how he will know that he will inherit this land, God asks him to prepare a sacrifice of three heifers, three goats, and three rams, a turtledove, and a young dove, and to cut them in halves. Abraham does as God commands but does not divide the young dove.

Birds of prey descend upon the carcasses and Abraham drives them away. As the sun is about to set, a deep sleep falls on Abraham. He is told that his descendants will be slaves in Egypt for four hundred years, and that the fourth generation of the people who enter Egypt will be freed and returned to this land (Genesis 16:13–16).

When the sun has set, there was a great darkness, and a torch of fire passed between the divided carcasses (Genesis 15:17). On that day, God enters into a covenant with Abraham in which he promises to give the land from the Nile River in Egypt to the Euphrates River to Abraham's descendants. Indeed, today the children of Abraham occupy this land from the Nile River to the Euphrates River; they include both Arabs and Jews, all of whom are Abraham's descendants.

It is not clear why God asks Abraham to divide the animals and then pass between the carcasses a torch of fire as a symbol of a covenant between them. This method of animal sacrifice does not match any of the sacrificial methods mentioned in Leviticus.

10.1 The birth of Ishmael

As time goes by and Sarah does not get pregnant, she gives Abraham the slave girl Hagar as a mate so that he will have children to continue his line and so that possibly Sarah herself will become pregnant, as often happens when women adopt babies (Genesis 16:2).

However, when Hagar gets pregnant, she becomes arrogant and considers Sarah an inadequate wife for Abraham. Sarah gets angry with Abraham and asks him to intervene on her behalf. Abraham tells Sarah that Hagar is her maid and she can do with her as she pleases. From that point on, Sarah starts to torture Hagar, and Hagar flees into the desert to escape from her.

Hagar is visited by an angel of God who promises Hagar that she will have a son and that her son will become the father of a great nation, and urges her to return to her mistress, Sarah. Indeed she returns to Sarah, and as time goes by she delivers a baby boy and calls him Ishmael (Genesis 16:11), meaning God has heard her suffering. Abraham is eighty-six years old when Ishmael is born.

10.2 The seven names of God

When Abraham is ninety-nine years old, God appears to him. This time God identifies himself as El-Shaddai (Genesis 17:1), and tells Abraham to walk before him and be perfect. God tells Abraham that he is entering into a covenant with him, that he will make Abraham the father of many nations, and that his name shall no longer be Abram but Abraham (Genesis 17:5). Abraham recognizes that this appearance by God is at a much higher level than his previous encounters, and he falls forward on his face to the ground as a sign of total respect (Genesis 17:3). Note that the name Abraham in Hebrew is spelled ם ה ר ב א, which is broken as ם -ה-ר-ב —א, and stands for "father

of many nations." The complete Hebrew statement is מַ ו ן ג ו י ם
אָ֭ב רְ ה ה. God also tells Abraham that this covenant will hold
true between God and Abraham's descendants forever. Furthermore,
he tells Abraham that he is changing Sarah's name from Sarai to Sarah
(Genesis 17:15). God has inserted the letter *hah*, ה, in both of their
names. Note that the letter ה is the connection between the first sefira,
Will, and the second sefira, Wisdom, or nothingness, as shown below.
The Zohar says that this letter represents the Holy Spirit.

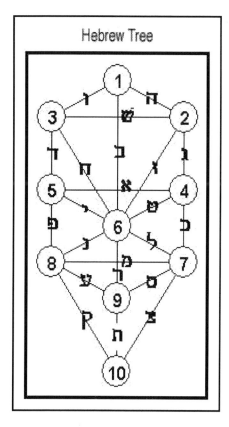

Hebrew Tree

This means that the original
light of God expressed by his
will to create the universe was
injected into both Abraham and
Sarah.

By this act, he caused both of
them to be enlightened, and
thereby they were ready to have
a child (Isaac), who was blessed
by God himself.

This injection of God's light
was necessary for Sarah to be
able to get pregnant at the age
of eighty-nine.

This tree is also known as the
Thirty-two Paths of Wisdom
and is derived from the Book of
Creation.

The name of God being identified here as El-Shaddai (Genesis 17:1) is significant and is one of the seven names of God. These names are given below. We will discuss each one separately.

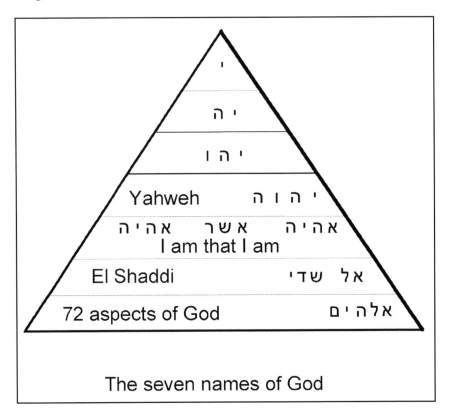

To start with, the name Yahweh (יהוה), which appears often in the Bible, is made up of four Hebrew letters, *yod, hah, vav,* and *hah*. The numerical equivalent of this name in Hebrew is twenty-six. That is also equal to the Hebrew letter *aleph,* (א), which is made from three different segments, *yod, vav,* and inverse *yod,* as can be seen above, giving again the number twenty-six.

The name of God, Yahweh, יהוה, is made up of four levels of creation, as shown below.

- The name of God, Yahweh, represents four levels of creation: *Atzilut* (Emanations or will), *Beriyah* (Creation), *Yetzirah* (Formation), and *Asiyah* (Making), discussed in the Zohar.

- These four levels of creation when put in the correct order form a triangle or pyramid. The head of the triangle is the letter *yod,* followed by the various levels, as shown below. Note that each side of the triangle yields the number seventy-two.

- Furthermore, when the triangle is constructed correctly, as shown below, we see that two of its sides have the same structure, whereas the third side has a different structure that is based on equal building blocks for each layer.

- Note that the two sides that have the same structure are separated by ninety degrees from each other in the same direction as the level of construction of each layer.

- The reader should follow the direction of the arrows that shows the electrical and magnetic fields.

All three corners of the triangle yield a total of seventy-two when the Hebrew letters and their numerical equivalents are used. Furthermore, both the left and the bottom sides of the triangle have the same structure when viewed from the top and right corners; they are therefore related to each other, but they are shifted by ninety degrees. This is the case in physics, when the electrical and the magnetic fields are at ninety degrees from each other. The third entity is gravity, and it has a different structure from the other two, as can be seen by viewing the triangle from the left corner.

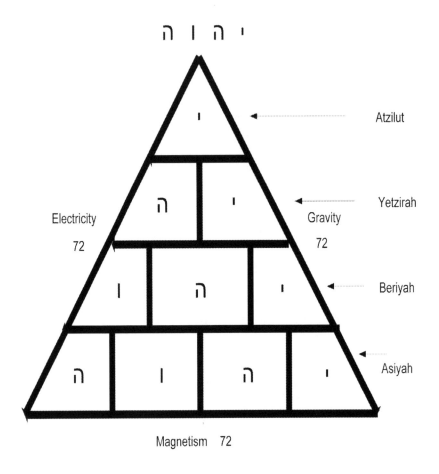

The 4 levels of existence

- Indeed, these two entities are related to each other through the laws of physics by ninety degrees, whereas the third entity, gravity, is based on a different structure.
- The structure of gravity is based on four levels of equal building blocks for each layer. Indeed, when gravity acts on matter, it will align the atomic structure in such a manner that the atomic structure of heavier elements will be at the bottom as we see in many of the planets' structures from the atmosphere to the core, including Earth's.

Let us now explore the other names for God as shown in the pyramid of the seven names of God.

When God appears to Abraham, in Genesis 17:1; to Isaac, in Genesis 28:3, even though Isaac only mentions him; and to Jacob, in Genesis 35:11, he identifies himself as El-Shaddai and not by any other name. However, when he appears to Moses, in Exodus 3:14, he identifies himself as אהיה אשר אהיה, or "I shall be as I shall be," and tells Moses that even though he has shown himself to Abraham, Isaac, and Jacob as El-Shaddai, his essence, which is Yahweh, has not been known to them (Exodus 6:3). In essence, he is telling Moses that there are several levels of revelations and that he can choose to appear to whomever he wishes.

Furthermore, as stated above, the name of Yahweh is more encompassing than El-Shaddai, and of "I am that I am." This is why God is telling Moses that what he revealed to Abraham, Isaac, and Jacob was not as much as he is revealing to Moses, which is the level of "I am that I am" of Yahweh.

Exodus 3:14 says, "And God said to Moses, I shall be as I shall be אהיה אשר אהיה and he said, so shall you say to the children of Israel, I shall be אהיה sent me to you."

There is another interpretation for "I shall be as I shall be," which is "I am that I am."

Let us examine what God says to Moses—"I am that I am," or "I shall be as I shall be"—and its meaning, and why he says that his inner name, Yahweh, was not known to any of the patriarchs.

Let us consider the first and the last word of the name of God as was told to Moses: *aleph, hah, yod,* and *hah* (אהיה). Their numerical equivalent is twenty-one each or forty-two together.

As discussed in chapter 5.1, the first letter in this word is *aleph,* א, which is made up of the ten dimensions and their opposites that created the universe and the separation between them. This first letter therefore means the universe itself.

The next three letters mean "existence" (היה), and their numerical equivalent is twenty. The Hebrew letter corresponding to twenty is *kaf,* כ; symbolically it is one half of a circle.

If we look carefully at the three words that are God's name, we observe that the first one and the last one are the same, meaning that the beginning and the end are the same, as explained earlier, in chapter 3.1.

Each of these two words contains half of a universe, and when combined they would create one whole universe and one complete circle. Indeed, the infinite, which has neither beginning nor end, is like a circle, which has neither beginning nor end.

The middle word, which is between these two words and inside the circle, is made up from three letters, *aleph, shin,* and *resh* (אשר). We have already discussed the meaning of the first letter, *aleph,* which means the universe itself. The second letter, *shin,* has three pillars, two of which two are derived from the same root, and the third one is by itself.

The reader should carefully examine the Hebrew letter *shin,* ש.

The first pillar of *shin,* which stands by itself, is the universal gravitational force, and the other two pillars are the magnetic and electrical forces of nature. These last two forces are related to each other and therefore derived from the same root.

This letter means that the universe was created with these three forces of nature.

The last letter, *resh,* derives its origin from the emanation of Knowledge, the third sefira, which is on the left side, and Wisdom or nothingness, or absolute uniformity, the second sefira, on the right side as shown in the diagram of the thirty-two paths of wisdom. It is with these two emanations and by using the three forces of nature that the universe is constructed. It is clear that wisdom and knowledge are needed to construct the universe, as was discussed earlier in Genesis, and that a balance, which is the sixth sefira from the top, must exist for the universe to exist, after the Creator or Good, the fourth sefira, and El-Shaddai or Might, the fifth sefira, who puts limits on the universe, completed the construction of the universe. The resulting structure beyond the sixth sefira from the top is the remaining four dimensions of time and space, known as space-time.

The location of the Hebrew letters in the Tree of Life as explained earlier is shown below.

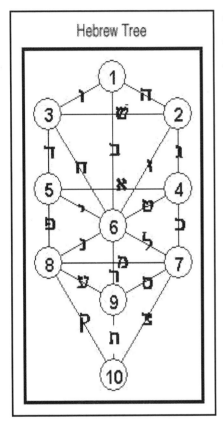

The second dimension is Wisdom or nothingness.

The third dimension is Knowledge.

The fourth dimension is the Creator or Good.

The fifth dimension is El-Shaddai, who places limits on the universe, or Might.

The sixth dimension is the balance required for the universe to exist.

Once the universe established a balance, the other four space-time dimensions can flow from it.

The letter ר flows from the sixth dimension from the top.

(from Wikipedia)

Let us consider the totality of the meaning of this name.

- Moses is told that the Creator, who is one, having no beginning or end—like a circle, which has no beginning and no end—has created the universe with wisdom and knowledge, using the three forces of nature.
- Moses was told that God's name "I am that I am" is infinite in nature.

- All the names of God that are mentioned in the Bible are descriptive in nature and serve to convey a specific aspect of the infinite.
- Human beings, being finite in nature, cannot comprehend the infinite, and therefore only specific aspects of the infinite are revealed to them.

We now understand what God revealed to Moses. It appears that he described to him who he was, the various levels of creation, the forces of nature that he used to construct the universe, and the exact structure of each force of nature.

Indeed, God acting on the one is all there is.

Therefore, the description of "I am that I am" is indeed a perfect description of God, and the meaning of the number seventy-two as mentioned in the Bible is now also clear.

Let us examine the name of God, El-Shaddai, which is made up of the letters *shin, dalet,* and *yod,* (' ז ש*)*. If one examines the name carefully, its numerical value is thirty-two. This is achieved by taking the three pillars of the letter *shin* to be equal to eighteen, with each one equal to six, or *vav;* the letter *dalet* as equal to four; and the letter *yod* as equal to ten. This provides the number thirty-two.

I have shown (in the tree of the thirty-two paths of wisdom derived directly from the Book of Creation mentioned earlier) that the universe was created with twenty-two letters of the Hebrew alphabet and ten numbers, which equals a total of thirty-two. I also mentioned that the exact construction of the universe and all within it was detailed by Abraham in his writing, which is two thousand words long and referred to as the Book of Creation. In this book, Abraham clearly describes the thirty-two paths of wisdom and then proceeds to describe each one and its effect on the universe. The reader should read the Book of Creation and its analysis by Rabbi Aryeh Kaplan to better understand the details of these thirty-two paths. I cannot describe the Book of Creation as explained by Rabbi Kaplan in this work because its description is more than three hundred pages long.

El-Shaddai is the Creator, the fifth sefira who placed boundaries on the universe through usage of letters and numbers. Indeed, many scholars regard the name El-Shaddai to mean the creator who put boundaries on the universe because of its last two letters, *dalet* and *yod*, which mean "enough" in Hebrew (ש-די). Note that God placed boundaries on the three forces of nature discussed above with the letter *shin*, שׁ, which implies that the universe is *not* infinite but rather finite. I believe the name El-Shaddai shows us directly what was used to place boundaries on the universe, as I explained above.

Let us examine the last name of God, which is made of seventy-two aspects or Elohim א ל ה י ם.

Each of these aspects is made up of three different letters or combinations. As discussed earlier, the name Yahweh yields a triangle where each side is made up of seventy-two variations. Furthermore, there are three different variations of the number seventy-two, according to Exodus 14:19–21. Therefore, there are seventy-two sets of three-letter combinations in total. These seventy-two combinations are the names of the seventy-two angels of God. I will prove that Elohim (א ל ה י ם), is an angel of God later in the book.

(from Wikipedia)

כהת	אכא	ללה	מהש	עלם	סיט	ילי	והו
הקם	הרי	מבה	יזל	ההע	לאו	אלד	הוי
חהו	מלה	ייי	נלך	פהל	כוו	בלי	לאו
ושר	לכב	אום	ריי	שאה	ירת	האא	נתה
ייז	רהע	חעם	אני	מנד	בוק	להח	יחו
כיה	עשל	ערי	סאל	ילה	וול	מיכ	ההה
פוי	מבה	נית	ננא	עמם	החש	דני	והו
כמי	ענו	יהה	וכב	מצר	הרח	ייל	נמם
כום	היי	יבם	ראה	חבו	איע	מנק	רמב

The seventy-two names of God

10.3 Abraham's circumcision covenant with God

In Genesis 17:10, God commands Abraham and all the males in his household to be circumcised as a covenant between God and Abraham for all generations. God also changes Sarah's name from Sarai to Sarah, promises Abraham that Sarah will give him a baby boy in one year's time (Genesis 17:21), and says that he will name him Isaac.

When Abraham hears God saying that Sarah will deliver a baby boy in one year's time, he laughs and says in his heart, "How could a hundred-year-old man and a ninety-year-old woman have a child?" (Genesis 17:17).

Abraham does not know the answer to this question, but because Ishmael is alive and thirteen years old, Abraham asks God to have Ishmael continue the covenant with him. However, God tells Abraham not to worry about Ishmael, because he will make Ishmael a mighty nation and the father of twelve presidents (Genesis 7:20). The meaning here is that twelve tribes will be born out of Ishmael, as in the case with Jacob.

God then tells Abraham that the covenant he established between himself and Abraham will continue through his son Isaac, who will be born in one year's time.

God promises Abraham that twelve tribes will be born out of Ishmael; however, we later see that Jacob, the son of Isaac, also has twelve children; they who become the twelve tribes of Israel.

What is the meaning of the twelve tribes, both from Ishmael and from Jacob through Isaac?

This is a difficult question. However, it is well known that in God's creation there is always a balance, and it is possible that the twelve tribes of Israel are to balance the twelve tribes of Ishmael. After all, Genesis 17:12 describes Ishmael as a wild ass of a man, whose hand will be against everyone and everyone's hand will be against. Later on, in Genesis 17:19, God tells Abraham that the covenant he made with him will continue through Isaac for all generations. It is therefore clear that when God gives his laws to the twelve tribes of Israel, he means that they will be the counterbalance for the twelve tribes of Ishmael. Whereas the children of Ishmael engage in fights with everyone, the children of Israel are meant to provide peace and the laws by which people should live, which indeed was the case. After this interaction between Abraham and God, Abraham has his entire household circumcised, including the servants who were bought with money.

10.4 Abraham and the three angels

Only after the circumcision of Abraham do the angels of God appear to him as men while he is recovering in his tent on the plains of Mamre (Genesis 18:2).

The oral tradition tells us that by the act of circumcision, Abraham is now fully purified and therefore able to be in the presence of God's angels.

Genesis 18:2 tells us that Abraham is startled to see three men standing in front of him. He becomes fearful and later runs toward them. Anyone who is familiar with the terrain of the city of Hebron and its surrounding area knows the land there is open and a person can see far. After all, the Bible tells us Abraham is sitting at the opening of his tent, which means he can see who is coming and going in front of him. Why then is Abraham startled and fearful when he sees three men standing?

If Abraham is startled, it means that the appearance of these three angels happens in an instant; otherwise he would have noticed them coming closer to his tent. This means they materialize suddenly, possibly at a very short distance. He is fearful, not knowing who they are, and later realizes that they are not ordinary men but angels of God. He runs toward them to welcome them into his tent to share food.

Abraham asks Sarah to prepare three meals and gives Ishmael a tender calf to prepare for his guests. He then gives the prepared food to his guests, who were seated next to the tree outside the tent to eat, while he stood to serve them (Genesis 18:8).

One of the angels asks him the whereabouts of Sarah, his wife (Genesis 18:9). This indicates that they know Sarah is his wife but not necessarily where she is. The angel tells Abraham that in one year's time Sarah will bear him a son (Genesis 18:10). When Sarah, standing inside the tent, hears this statement from the angel, she laughs to herself, saying in her heart, "Now, when I no longer have a period and my master is old? How could that be?" (Genesis 18:12).

Her thoughts seem to be heard by the angel, because he immediately asks Abraham why Sarah laughed and asked how she could deliver at her age. Is anything too hard for God? (Genesis 18:13–14).

When Sarah hears the angel answering the question that she is thinking to herself, she becomes fearful and denies the answer the angel gives her. However, the angel insists that she did indeed laugh, in Genesis 18:15. Note here that even though it says that Yahweh speaks to Abraham about Sarah's laughter, it is done through one of the angels.

Also note that God's actions have multiple purposes. In this case, the angels come to notify Abraham of the birth of Isaac and to destroy Sodom and Gomorrah at the same time. We have birth on one hand and destruction on the other. A balance has been struck.

Note also that three angels come to Abraham, whereas only two continue on to destroy Sodom and Gomorrah. Oral tradition tells us that these three angels were Michael, Gabriel, and Raphael. However, only Gabriel and Raphael went on to destroy Sodom and Gomorrah.

Chapter 11   The Destruction of Sodom and Gomorrah and the Story of Lot

Genesis 18:22 says that the other angels, "men," continued toward Sodom while Abraham was still standing in front of Yahweh. This sentence shows us that only two of the three angels continued to Sodom and the third one was with Abraham. This third angel, speaking for Yahweh, says to Abraham that the sin of Sodom is great. The scream that reached him caused him to come down to check. If the scream is justified, he will destroy the city, and if it is not justified, he will know (Genesis 18:21).

Here again God is using angels to do his will. Furthermore, it appears that he sends these angels to check the cause of the scream that resulted from the suffering inflicted on various victims. He aims to find out the truth, as he did with the Tower of Babel, and later when the people of Israel screamed to him because of their suffering under Egyptian rule, in Exodus 2:23.

When Abraham hears this angel telling him about the sin of Sodom, he worries, knowing that Lot, his nephew, is living in Sodom. He then approaches the angel and starts to plead his case for saving the righteous among the people of Sodom, in Genesis 18:23.

God, knowing what Abraham is trying to do, agrees that if there are fifty righteous people in Sodom, he will spare the entire city on their behalf (Genesis 18:26). Knowing that it may be difficult to find fifty righteous people in Sodom, Abraham tries to bargain with God until he lowers the number to ten, in Genesis 18:32.

Once Abraham is satisfied that he cannot ask God to spare Sodom even if there aren't ten righteous people within it, God leaves Abraham, and Abraham returns to his tent (Genesis 18:33). Even though the Bible does not detail the means that God will use to destroy Sodom, some information must have been provided to Abraham during this conversation, because Abraham's actions after the destruction of these cities is a clear indication that he knew the kind of weapons used to destroy the cities, as we shall see shortly.

Meanwhile, the other two "men," now identified as angels (Genesis 19:1), continue to Sodom.

Lot, sitting at the city gate, sees them coming and immediately recognizes them as angels of God. He therefore falls down on his face as one would bow to a king (Genesis 19:1).

He asks them to accompany him to his house so that they can spend the night, wash their feet, and in the morning continue on their journey. However, they refuse, saying they will sleep on the street (Genesis 19:2). After much insistence by Lot, they agree to accompany him to his house.

At Lot's house, he bakes them bread and brings them drinks. Before they are able to sleep on their beds, the entire population of Sodom, from a young boy to the city's eldest, assembles in front of the house, in Genesis 19:4.

The crowd demands that Lot bring these men outside so that they could have sex with them (Genesis 19:5).

Lot exits the house and closes the door behind him. He tries to reason with the people of Sodom, saying that these men are guests in his house and should be left alone and not be harmed. However, if sex is what people want, then he has two young virgin daughters he will give them, and they can do with them whatever they wish (Genesis 19:8).

Lot knows the people of Sodom are not interested in his two daughters, since they were seeking homosexual contact; therefore he does not hesitate to offer them to the crowd. However, he is told, "Get out of here. The one who came to live among us has now became a judge over us; judge now for we will harm you for these men," and they try to break the door of the house (Genesis 19:9).

At this point, the two angels grab Lot, pull him inside the house, and close the door behind him, and they hit the people in front of the house with great light that causes them to be temporarily blind, the same effect as when one looks directly at the sun (Genesis 19:11).

Then the two angels ask Lot if he has sons-in-law, sons, daughters, or anyone else who is his, and tells them to get out of the city, for they are going to destroy it (Genesis 19:12–13).

This statement shows again, as was discussed in regard to Sarah, that the angels do not know who belongs to Lot and where they are.

Lot does as the angels ask: he leaves the house and tries to speak to his future sons-in-law, those men who are engaged to his daughters. However, they laugh at him and consider him like a jester (Genesis 19:14).

As the sun is about to rise, the two angels urge Lot to take his wife and two daughters who were with him in the house and leave the city at once so that he and his family will be spared and not killed for the sin of Sodom (Genesis 19:15).

However, Lot is not fast enough, so the two angels hold two people each: one holds Lot and his wife, and the other holds his two daughters, bringing them out of the city and putting them down on the ground outside the city (Genesis 19:16).

This sentence shows us that these two angels used teleportation technology to bring Lot and his family from inside the city and its walls to its outskirts. Note that the Bible says that "they put them down outside the city," meaning they were transferred through the air.

Furthermore, by holding onto their hands, they were able to travel together through the air.

Once Lot and his family are outside the city walls, the angels tell them to run for their lives to the mountains across the valley in order to survive, and not to look back (Genesis 19:17).

However, Lot pleads with the angels, for he knows that he cannot make it to the mountains before sunrise, and he asks to go to the nearby city of Zoar, which is one of the five cities on the plain surrounding the Dead Sea.

The angels grant him his wish and do not start the destruction of Sodom and Gomorrah until Lot makes it to Zoar.

At sunrise, God rains sulfur and fire on Sodom and Gomorrah and turns the entire fertile valley upside down, destroying everything, including all the plants of the Earth (Genesis 19:25).

So intense is the fire that when Abraham looks over Sodom and Gomorrah the next morning, all he can see is a fire like an oven (Genesis 19:28).

In destroying Sodom and Gomorrah and all the cities of the plain surrounding the Dead Sea of today, God remembers his discussion with Abraham about the killing of the righteous in Sodom, and he saves Lot by allowing him to escape from Zoar into one of the caves in the nearby mountains, according to (Genesis 19:29). It appears that Lot's wife did not obey the advice of the angels, and we are told that she has turned into a statue of salt.

Once Lot has seen the destruction of Sodom and Gomorrah, he is afraid to stay in the city of Zoar, and he climbs into the mountains and hides inside a cave with his daughters. He realizes that the cave can offer shelter from all these bombardments from the sky. Indeed, his daughters, observing that the entire valley of the Dead Sea has been wiped out, including all the cities within it, think that all life on Earth has been destroyed and that no other living soul besides them is still alive. The level of destruction must have been enormous. Indeed, we are told that the Jordan Valley before the destruction was as lush as the Garden of Eden planted by God and as lush as the Nile delta of Egypt, which was known for its fertile land (Genesis 13:10).

They therefore take an extraordinary measure to ensure that the human species continues (Genesis 19:31). They give their father lots of wine to make him unaware of the sexual act they are planning. Indeed, the elder of Lot's daughters is the first to sleep with her father and be impregnated by him, and the younger one does the same thing the following night, according to Genesis 19:33 and 35.

It is clear that this act is totally forbidden and that they know that. However, because they think all life around them has been wiped out, they decide to perform this unnatural and extreme act of survival. The descendants of these two daughters of Lot are rejected by God. They become the nations of Moab and Ammon, according to Genesis 19:36–37.

Chapter 12   Abraham and King Abimelech of Gerar

Genesis 20:1 tells us that Abraham leaves his residence in Hebron and moves to the city of Gerar, which is not far from today's Gaza, after the destruction of the cities of Sodom and Gomorrah.

The destruction must have been so enormous that even Abraham did not want to be anywhere close to these sites after seeing the destruction of these cities the next morning (Genesis 19:27–28). Note that the blast radius of a half-a-megaton nuclear bomb is eight to thirteen miles. Hebron was outside that radius; however, the radiated area can be much larger than that, possibly thirty to forty miles from ground zero. In addition to a potential nuclear bomb, the valley of Siddim was also bombarded with sulfur-based bombs that destroyed all plant life in the valley. The sulfur cloud must have traveled a great distance and reached Abraham, who was living in Hebron, some fifteen to twenty miles away from the valley.

The question of why Abraham leaves his residence in Hebron, which he loved, and moves all the way to Gerar, about sixty miles from Sodom, may explain the kind of weapons used on Sodom, Gomorrah, and the other cities. It appears that Abraham knew the destructive power of these bombs, their radius of radioactive fallout, and the effect of the sulfur-based bombs. Even after he moves to Gerar at the age of ninety-nine, he does not return to Hebron to settle there, and returns only after about thirty years, possibly knowing that the area is still contaminated with radioactivity. The table below shows the half-life of most radioactive isotopes.

Half-lives of radioactive isotopes (www.iem-inc.com).

Uranium

- U-232 - 72 years

Strontium

- Sr-90 - 29.12 years

Radium

- Ra-228 - 5.75 years

Plutonium

- Pu-238 - 87.74 years
- Pu-241 - 14.4 years
- Ra-228 - 5.75 years

Niobium

- Nb-93m - 13.6 years

Nickel

- Ni-63 - 96 years

Lead

- Pb-210 - 22.3 years

Krypton

- Kr-85 - 10.72 years

Iron

- Fe-55 - 2.7 years

Hydrogen

- H-3 - 12.35 years

Europium

- Eu-152 - 13.33 years
- Eu-154 - 8.8 years
- Eu-155 - 4.96 years

Curium

- Cm-243 - 28.5 years
- Cm-244 - 18.11 years

Cesium

- Cs-134 - 2.062 years
- Cs-137 - 30.0 years

Californium

- Cf-252 - 2.638 years

Cadmium

- Cd-113m - 13.6 years

Antimony

- Sb-125 - 2.77 years

Actinium

- Ac-227 - 21.773 years

(end of article)

Note that all these radioactive isotopes have a half-life of less than thirty years, and only three have half-lives of less than ninety years. We know that Abraham travels to Hebron to buy the burial lot for Sarah thirty-seven years after he moves to Gerar. This means that most of the radioactivity of the isotopes listed above would have disappeared.

Furthermore, the angels tell Lot that he should seek shelter in one of the caves in the mountain near Sodom. This advice explains the reason for that suggestion. The angels know the radiation from such a nuclear bombardment means radioactive fallout, and if Lot is inside a mountain cave, he will not be harmed. Also, they warn Lot not to look back, knowing that the radiation burns that may be caused from the nuclear blast will cause death from horrible blisters. We saw such a phenomenon in Hiroshima and Nagasaki, Japan, during World War II.

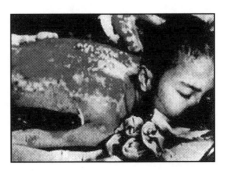

A photograph of Sumiteru Taniguchi's back injuries taken in January 1946 by a US Marine photographer

(from Wikipedia.org)

Note that the back of this victim was toward the atomic blast, whereas her face was away from it. This photo clearly shows that if the flesh is exposed to the blast, it will burn, depending on the person's distance from ground zero. However, if the flesh is not directly exposed to the atomic blast, it will survive pretty much intact. This may be what happens to Lot's wife when she disobeys the command of the angels and looks back on the blast from the sky in Genesis 19:26. Note that the sulfur-based bombs were intended mainly for the plant life in the valley of Siddim. The explanation given here suggests that two types of weapons were used on Sodom, Gomorrah, and the other cities of the valley of Siddim.

The fact that Zoar is destroyed only after Sodom and then Gomorrah gives Lot and his family time to escape into the nearby mountains and hide in one of the caves there.

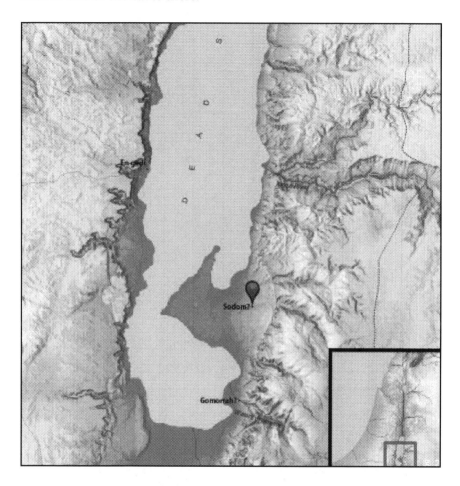

When Abraham comes to live among the people of Gerar, in Genesis 20:1, it is out of necessity rather than desire, since it is clear that he loved the Hebron area and it would have taken a great negative event to make him leave it. We see that Abraham returns and buys a burial lot for Sarah and for himself in Hebron in Genesis 24:17–18. This indicates that he does not want the two of them to be buried anywhere else.

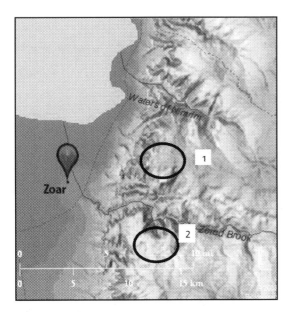

These are the mountains closest to the city of Zoar.

Location 1 is the more likely place for the cave in which Lot hid with his two daughters.

The distance from Zoar to location 1 is about five miles and can be reached in a little over an hour.

When Abraham comes to the city of Gerar, he is worried that its people do not fear God and therefore are lawless and might kill him in order to possess Sarah. Sarah is now eighty-nine years old and by her own admission thinks of herself as an old woman (Genesis 18:12–13). Still he asks her to say that she is his sister and not his wife, as he did before in Egypt.

It seems that Abimelech, king of Gerar, sends men to take Sarah from the house of Abraham without asking Abraham's permission, because they believe he is her brother (Genesis 20:2).

Genesis 20:3 tells us that God appears to Abimelech in a dream during the night and warns him that he will be punished by the death of all that is his if he does anything to Sarah, because she is the wife of a man called Abraham and that he is a prophet of God (Genesis 20:7).

This is the first time in Genesis that the word *prophet* is used. What is meant by this word is that Abraham can see into the future. This is an important admission by God that Abraham has the ability to see into the future, which explains why he was able to figure out God's creation, as discussed earlier.

The reasons for the selection of Abraham for the covenant with God are discussed in chapter 10. He was the first person since the early generations of Adam to figure out God's creation. This ability to see the future was passed on to Isaac, Jacob, and Joseph, as we shall see shortly.

Genesis 20:8 tells us that Abimelech woke up in the morning, summoned his court advisers, and notified them about his dream, and they all became fearful. This is understandable, since Abraham was a newcomer to their city and they did not know him at all.

Thereafter, Abimelech summons Abraham and asks him why he did such a thing, saying that Sarah is his sister when in fact she is his wife.

Abraham tells Abimelech he was fearful that Gerar is lawless and that the people might kill him in order to possess Sarah (Genesis 20:11).

However, Abraham explains to Abimelech that he and Sarah have the same father but different mothers (Genesis 20:12), and that he asks her to say that she is his sister whenever they come to a new place in order to protect himself from being killed on account of her beauty.

Note that the issue between Sarah and King Abimelech of Gerar is the same one that arose between Sarah and Pharaoh. However, Sarah is now eighty-nine and not sixty-five, as she was at the time of the incident with Pharaoh. Again we ask how this is possible. Why would a king take an old lady as a potential wife unless she looked not like an old woman but rather like a young one?

The reason for this phenomenon is explained earlier, and indeed this passage shows us that Sarah did not age.

This passage further demonstrates that both Abraham and Sarah were not affected by time, and remained young looking. This is an important lesson. It shows that contact with advanced beings or angels causes humans not to be affected by time. Now we can understand why holy people, meaning those who came in contact with advanced beings or angels, remained intact as far as their physical appearance, even after many hundreds of years passed and even though they were buried in the ground.

Chapter 13   The Birth of Isaac

Genesis 21:2 tells us about the birth of Isaac. Abraham circumcises the boy when he is eight days old according to God's command (Genesis 21:4). So unusual is the birth of Isaac to Sarah at her age that even she says that anyone hearing that she has delivered a baby will laugh at her (Genesis 21:6). However, as the boy grows up, it appears that Ishmael is making fun of him (Genesis 21:9). This causes Sarah to be angry, and she demands that Abraham banish Hagar from their house. Abraham does not like this idea and is very angry, in Genesis 21:11. After all, Sarah has asked him to banish his other son, which is impossible for any father to do.

Seeing the difficulty Abraham is in, God intervenes and tells him to listen to Sarah and do as she says, since only through Isaac will his covenant be fulfilled. He also tells Abraham that he intends to make Ishmael a nation, since he is from Abraham's seed, (Genesis 21:13).

The next morning, Abraham sends Hagar and her son Ishmael out of the camp and into the desert of Beersheba, carrying sufficient food and water for several days. As Hagar goes into the desert, she loses her way and runs out of water and food. She places the child under a bush for shade so that he will not be dehydrated and then sits crying at a distance, for she does not want to see him die in front of her eyes (Genesis 21:16).

Again, an angel of God intervenes and shows her a well of water so that she and the child can drink from it and survive (Genesis 21:19). The Bible continues and says that God is with the boy and he grows to be an archer. Hagar takes an Egyptian woman to be a mate for her son, and he settles in the desert of Paran (Genesis 21:21).

Note that God, El-Shaddai, tells Abraham that his son Ishmael will beget twelve presidents, and that he will become a great nation (Genesis 17:20). This means that Ishmael has twelve children who become twelve tribes. Later, Jacob, the son of Isaac, also has twelve children who become the twelve tribes of Israel.

Note that the word נשיאם in Hebrew means "presidents or head of nations," or "tribes" as mentioned in Numbers 13:2–3.

Why was there a need to have two sets of twelve tribes?

We know that God tells Hagar when she runs away from Sarah's torture, in Genesis 16:6, that she will have a baby boy and should call him Ishmael (Genesis 16:11). However, the angel says he will be a wild ass of a man, his hand against everyone and everyone's hands against him (Genesis 16:12).

Later, we find that another set of twelve children is born to Jacob, and they become the twelve tribes of Israel.

The reason for these two sets of twelve tribes has to do with the balance described in chapter 3.4 above. However, God chooses the children of Isaac and Jacob to be the ones receiving his laws over the children of Ishmael. The reason given by the angel to Hagar explains why the children of Isaac and Jacob were chosen (Genesis 16:12). The children of Ishmael are the tribes of the Sinai Desert, which was part of the Egyptian kingdom.

13.1   The covenant of Abraham and King Abimelech

Genesis 21:22 tells us that King Abimelech of Gerar travels to Beersheba together with the head of his army, Phicol, to see Abraham. Abimelech wants to make sure Abraham will not curse him or his people, because he knows God is with Abraham, having been told in a dream that Abraham is a prophet of God. This means that if Abraham blesses or curses a person, that blessing or curse will occur.

When they meet, Abimelech asks Abraham to "do kindness" with him and his descendants up to the fourth generation, as he did to Abraham (Genesis 21:23). Knowing that Abraham has lied to him before, when he said Sarah was his sister, he asks Abraham to swear to him by God that he will not lie to him. Abraham agrees; however, he tells Abimelech that his servant has robbed him of one of the wells that he dug for the herds. Abimelech immediately apologizes and tells Abraham he does not know who did this thing, that Abraham himself did not tell him before, and that he is hearing about this event only now (Genesis 21:26).

Abraham then takes cattle and sheep and gives them to King Abimelech (Genesis 21:27). This gesture is meant as an exchange for the well he will now own from Abimelech. Abraham does not want to take anything from Abimelech that he does not pay for, including the well.

He then takes seven sheep and isolates them from the rest, according to Genesis 21:28. When King Abimelech asks him why he has separated the seven sheep and placed them by themselves, Abraham tells him that these seven sheep will be witnesses between them that he has dug the well that the servants of Abimelech have taken from him and that he has now paid for. They both enter into a covenant, and King Abimelech returns to the land of the Philistines. The place where they enter into a covenant is known as Beersheba, or the Well of Seven (Genesis 21:31).

Abraham plants an "Eshel," a kind of tree, at that place, and he then calls in the name of Yahweh, "El Olam," or "God of the universe" (Genesis 21:33).

Let us examine Abraham's actions.

- He takes seven sheep and used them as a witness for the covenant between him and King Abimelech that gives the well to Abraham after he pays for it with cattle and sheep. The reason for the seven sheep is that Abraham wants to ensure that all seven levels of the divine witness this covenant. These seven levels have been explained earlier as the lower seven sefirot.

- Once they enter into a covenant, he plants an "Eshel" tree and calls in the name of Yahweh, "El Olam," meaning God of the universe. This shows us that Abraham knew of the existence of the ten dimensions of the universe and its lower seven dimensions, which manifested themselves as physical creation.

He did not say, "Elohim" (א ל ה י ם), "El-Shaddai," or any other name, but appealed directly to the divine one that is the God of the entire universe, which is the seventh level of the divine as discussed in chapter 10.2 above. The planting of the tree is meant to mark the location of the well, and because the well is now his, there is sufficient water to plant a tree next to it. We will see later in Genesis that Jacob knows about this tree and the well as he plans to move to Egypt (Genesis 46:1).

13.2 Abraham and Isaac are tested by God

Genesis 22:1 tells us that God decides to test Abraham. The Bible continues with the story of the attempted sacrifice of Isaac, in Genesis chapter 22. It is clear that this is a test by God to ensure that Abraham, Isaac, and their children are worthy to receive God's laws that he will bestow on them.

It is not sufficient that Abraham is faithful and loyal to God; the test God has prepared is for both of them. In this way, God is testing Abraham and Isaac at the same time. Note that the test he chooses is the most severe that can be asked of any father: to sacrifice the son God gave him after a hundred years—his miracle child. However, Abraham understands that it was God who gave him Isaac through Sarah even though she was eighty-nine years old. Therefore, if God orders him now to sacrifice that same child, his will shall be done.

Isaac, after seeing that there is no lamb to be used as sacrifice (Genesis 22:7), understands that he will be the sacrifice to God, and yet he continues with his father toward the sacrificial place and allows his father to tie him up as a sacrificial lamb.

This shows that both men accept the commandment of God. In doing so, God is assured that both Abraham and Isaac are worthy to be his chosen people and to receive his laws. The test continues until the last second before Abraham's blade would cut into Isaac's flesh, according to Genesis (22:10). This is done in order to be sure that neither Abraham nor Isaac changes their mind. Indeed, this shows the absolute trust and loyalty of both men in God. Note that Isaac is a grown man at this point and quite capable of resisting Abraham if he wants to.

Chapter 14   Hebron and the Cave of Machpelah

Genesis 23:1 tells us that Sarah lives to be 127 years old and that she dies in the city of Hebron in the land of Canaan. This means that Abraham has returned to Hebron after living at Beersheba for many years. Note that the distance from Beersheba to Hebron is about twenty-five miles in a straight line. This statement confirms what was said earlier in regard to Abraham moving out of Hebron because of the destruction of Sodom and Gomorrah and the entire valley of Siddim, and the weapons that were used there. Also, in appealing to the people of Hebron to sell him a burial plot, Abraham says he is an immigrant and a resident of Hebron (Genesis 23:4). He must therefore have returned to Hebron and lived among the people there, and possibly still maintains a residence in Beersheba, which was not that far away.

Remember that the half-life of most radioactive materials that were on the list in chapter 12 is less than thirty years, which is the amount of time that Abraham stayed out of this area.

Genesis 23 describes Sarah's death and burial in the cave of Machpelah. There are several points that I want to discuss here. The first one is about the price paid for the cave and the land surrounding it.

Note that Abraham pays four hundred shekels of silver to purchase the land and the cave, according to Genesis 23:16. He then buries Sarah in the cave of Machpelah. The word *Machpelah* means "double." What the Bible is telling us is that this cave has two chambers. Oral tradition tells us that Abraham, Isaac, Jacob, and their wives were buried in the first chamber of the cave, and the inner chamber contained the bodies of Adam and Eve. Abraham knows that. That is why he insists on buying this specific cave from the people of Hebron. Note that Ephron the Hittite asked four hundred shekels for the cave (Genesis 23:15).

We encounter the number four hundred in various places in the Bible, all of them having to do with evil. The people of Israel are enslaved for four hundred years in Egypt. Jezebel, the wife of King Ahab of Israel and the daughter of King Ethbaal of Sidon, who worshipped Baal—Satan—has four hundred priests of darkness in her temple in Megiddo whom she provides with food and shelter and who serve her, according to Kings 18:19.

Esau comes to meet Jacob with four hundred men after Jacob crosses the Jordan River into Israel, in Genesis 33:1. Esau's intent is clear: he is going to kill his brother for stealing his birthright from his father, Isaac. In fact, the Bible says that Esau declares that after his father's death, he will take revenge on Jacob by killing him (Genesis 27:41).

In all these three instances, the number four hundred indicates evil deeds. By buying the land and the cave from the people of Hebron, who are Hittites and descendants of Canaan, whom Noah cursed for his wickedness, Abraham is in fact releasing the hold of evil on the cave in exchange for four hundred shekels of silver. The other issue is that of the double chambers in the cave. As stated earlier, oral tradition tells us that the inner room is where the bodies of Adam and Eve are buried, according to the Zohar.

One might wonder why Adam and Eve are buried in Hebron and not in Mesopotamia. Is it possible that God has directed Abraham to the land of Israel because of this? We know that after Adam is banished from the Garden of Eden, which, as I said before, is in southeast Turkey, in the region where the Tigris and Euphrates Rivers originate, around the region of the city of Van, Adam settles in the region of

Mesopotamia. How then is it possible that Adam and Eve were buried in Hebron?

The answer to this question is as follows: Even though Jacob and later Joseph both die in Egypt, a long distance away from Hebron, they are carried all the way to Hebron and Shechem to be buried, according to Genesis 50:13. This shows us that the place of death is not as important as the place of burial. Indeed, by this logic, it is quite possible that both Adam and Eve were buried in Hebron.

Oral tradition dating back to the first century CE tells us that the inner chamber of the cave had an opening that led to the Garden of Eden (Zohar).

After Abraham buries Sarah, he takes another woman, who bears him six children (Genesis 25:1–2). Abraham lives another thirty-eight years after Sarah's death. However, in order not to create conflict among his children, he gives Isaac all that he has, then gives gifts to his other children, and sends all of them to the east, according to Genesis 25:6. It is possible that many of the Eastern religions originated from the knowledge given to these children.

Abraham dies when he is 175 years old, according to Genesis 25:7. Both Isaac and Ishmael bury him in the cave of Machpelah, where Sarah is buried (Genesis 25:9). We do not know the burial place of Hagar, but it must be in the Sinai Desert of Paran. Genesis 25:16 repeats the statement that God has made to Abraham about Ishmael and his twelve sons—that they will become presidents of nations, as we explained earlier.

Chapter 15   The Story of Isaac

After Sarah's death and burial at Hebron, Abraham decides to seek a wife for his son Isaac. Isaac is now about 40 years old, and Abraham is about 140. Abraham wants to take a wife for Isaac from his family, now that his brother Nahor has many children from Milcah (Genesis 22:20) and they have sons and daughters. Nahor's youngest son, Bethuel, has a daughter by the name of Rebecca (Genesis 22:23).

He therefore asks his loyal servant, Eliezer, who is in charge of all his affairs, to travel to the land of his fathers and take a wife for his son Isaac (Genesis 24:4). The Bible says Abraham's servant is Eliezer from Damascus.

Abraham asks his servant to swear to him that he will not take a wife for his son Isaac from the land of Canaan. To complete this swearing, Abraham asks Eliezer to place his hand under his right thigh (Genesis 24:2). This is a well-known gesture that was used until 1951 among the Jews of Babylon who returned from Iraq to Israel in May of that year.

Today, we are asked to place a hand on the Bible to swear to tell the truth. In Abraham's time, one was asked to place his hand under the other person's thigh, typically the right thigh, since the left thigh has become sacrilege, as discussed later in the story of Jacob. Abraham further instructs Eliezer not to take Isaac a wife from Canaan, even if he does not find a wife for Isaac from Abraham's former land (Genesis 24:8).

In any event, Eliezer travels to the city of Haran in search of a suitable wife for Isaac. Genesis 24:10 tells us that Eliezer takes ten camels loaded with all kinds of fine goods and gifts to be used as a dowry when he locates the right woman. When he arrives at the outskirts of the city, he makes the camels kneel next to a well of water from which the people draw their water (Genesis 24:11).

When he sees Rebecca drawing water from the well, he asks her for water to drink, and she obliges him and continues to draw water for his camels. The Bible tells us that this is the sign that Abraham's servant has asked God for, so that he will be able to tell which woman is the right one for Isaac (Genesis 24:12–14). Indeed, his prayer is accepted, and Rebecca is the girl who meets this condition (Genesis 24:18–19). However, the Bible calls Rebecca (ה נ ע ר) (Genesis 24:14, 16, 28, 55, 57), which does not include ה at the end of the word the way the spelling of a young woman should be, נ. ע ר ה.

Why does the Bible use the word for "young lady" but without the letter *hah* in Hebrew for Rebecca? It appears that if the letter ה is missing from the description of a young woman, it means this woman is missing something. Indeed, we find out later that Rebecca is not able to have children (Genesis 25:21); since she is barren. It is therefore not an accident that the Bible does not have a complete description of a young woman that includes the letter *hah* when he describes Rebecca. Only after Isaac intervenes and prays to God to allow Rebecca to have children, in Genesis 25:21, does Rebecca get pregnant with Jacob and Esau.

Genesis 24:22–62 recounts the story of Rebecca. Eliezer tells both Laban, Rebecca's brother, and Bethuel, her father, about the task that his master, Abraham, has tasked him with, and how he has asked God to show him the right woman for Isaac by setting up a condition that Rebecca fulfills completely, which answers his prayer.

Both Laban and Bethuel agree that the events that took place are from God and that they have no objection to Rebecca becoming Isaac's wife. They ask for ten more days to be with her before she is allowed to leave (Genesis 24:55). However, Eliezer tells Laban that they should not delay him in the fulfillment of his mission. Both Laban and Bethuel decide to ask Rebecca if she wishes to leave immediately. When they ask her, she says she will go with Eliezer (Genesis 24:58). So they send her, together with her maids, on her way (Genesis 24:61).

The Bible tells us in Genesis 24:62 that Isaac has just returned from Beer Lahai, which is in the Negev Desert. Toward evening of that same day, he goes out to take a walk in the fields when he sees a caravan of camels, (Genesis 24:63).

When he meets the caravan, Eliezer tells Isaac all that has taken place, and that is when he meets Rebecca. The Bible tells us that Isaac loves Rebecca and takes her for a wife. It appears that Isaac is residing at Beersheba when this takes place.

Genesis 25:1 says that Abraham takes another wife by the name of Keturah. Rashi says that this woman is the Egyptian Hagar. This is not likely since Hagar would have been more than seventy years old, and for her to deliver six boys, a task that would take at minimum twelve years, making her at least eighty-two years old, was nearly impossible.

Furthermore, we know that for Sarah to get pregnant at the age of eighty-nine required God's intervention; for Hagar to have six more children after she delivered Ishmael fifty-four years earlier seems unlikely. Therefore, when the Bible says the name of this new woman was Keturah, indeed she was not Hagar. We get more assurance from the fact that Abraham sends these new children to the east after giving them gifts, (Genesis 25:6). If this woman was Hagar, then the children would be sent to Egypt and the west.

Genesis 25:8–9 tells us that when Abraham died, both his children, Isaac and Ishmael, buried him in the cave of Machpelah in Hebron together with Sarah.

After the death of his father, Isaac moves to Beer Lahai from Beersheba (Genesis 25:11), and he lived there for many years.

Genesis 25:21 says that Rebecca was barren and could not have children until Isaac entreated God. Only then does Rebecca become pregnant. When she finds out she is pregnant with twins, and that these twins are chasing each other in her womb, she seeks the advice of God, (Genesis 25:22). We do not know whom Rebecca sees, but the Bible says that God has told her that two nations will be born out of her and that the older one will serve the younger one (Genesis 25:23).

This advice from God lays the groundwork for Rebecca to persuade Jacob to lie to his father, Isaac, so that he might receive the blessing of the firstborn son. It is not Jacob who wants to lie to his father but Rebecca, and she is so sure about God's advice that she tells Jacob that if Isaac curses him instead of blessing him, that curse will be on her (Genesis 27:13).

The sale of the birthright by Esau to Jacob over some red lentil soup and a piece of bread (Genesis 25:33–34), is not known to Rebecca and is not the reason she encourages Jacob to seek the blessing from his father, Isaac. After all, the selling of the right of the firstborn happens between the two boys, and no divine being is involved with the sale, other than the swearing that Jacob insists on to seal the deal (Genesis 25:33). We don't know what is said between them, and by whose name Esau swears.

15.1   Isaac and King Abimelech of Gerar

Genesis 26:1 tells us there is a severe famine in the land, and Isaac is forced to go back to the city of Gerar, where Abraham lived for many years and Isaac lived for some time. Isaac knows that being near a large city will allow him to survive the famine. It appears that the Middle East had a cycle of famine every 100–110 years.

This cycle of famine is derived from the first famine that the Bible mentions at the time of Abraham, when he had just come into Canaan from Haran. He was forced to seek food in Egypt, as was discussed earlier. Abraham was around seventy-five to seventy-seven years old at that point. Again, when Isaac is around seventy-six to eighty, another famine occurs in the land. The third famine occurs at the time of Jacob, which causes Jacob to seek food in Egypt (Genesis 42:1).

The time frame between these three events is about 100–110 years. This is possibly why in our day, the phrase "100 years' event" for catastrophic events such as flood, famine, or other natural disasters is used.

Genesis 26:25 tells us that God shows himself to Isaac and tells him to stay in Gerar and not to go to Egypt, and that he will be with him in this land. This means that Isaac was making preparation to go to Egypt in order to survive.

Knowing that his wife, Rebecca, is a very good-looking woman, even at the age of around fifty-two to fifty-six, and with twins about eighteen to twenty years old, Isaac repeats the strategy of his father, Abraham, by telling the people of Gerar that Rebecca is his sister rather than his wife, out of fear for his life (Genesis 26:7).

After Isaac has lived in Gerar for some time, King Abimelech of Gerar, the same Abimelech who tried to take Sarah for a wife during Abraham's stay in Gerar, is looking out the window of his palace and sees Isaac being playful with Rebecca not as a brother, but as a husband (Genesis 26:8).

Having the same experience with Sarah and Abraham, and knowing the consequences if something were to happen to Rebecca, he summons Isaac immediately to his palace (Genesis 26:9).

He asks Isaac why Isaac said Rebecca is his sister when in fact she is his wife.

Isaac uses the same excuse as Abraham, saying he was afraid for his life because of his wife's beauty (Genesis 26:9). In the next verse, King Abimelech is angry with him and asks what would happen if one of the people of the city slept with Rebecca and brought guilt over his house.

After this incident, Abimelach commands all his people not to approach or touch Rebecca, for they risk being punished by death (Genesis 26:11).

The Bible tells us that Isaac becomes a very wealthy man (Genesis 26:13). This wealth obviously causes jealousy among the people of Gerar (Genesis 26:14). As a result of this jealousy, the Philistines clog all the wells that Abraham dug and owned, including the well of Sheba. At this point, King Abimelech tells Isaac to get out of his land, because he has become very rich and powerful (Genesis 26:16).

Isaac is forced to leave Gerar and move to the valley of Gerar (Genesis 26:17). He then digs the same wells that Abraham dug in his days and that Isaac knew from his youth (Genesis 26:18), and he names them the same names his father did.

Isaac tries to dig new wells that the Philistines claim to be theirs, until they force him to move all the way back to Rehoboth, where he digs a well and finds water, far enough away that they do not bother him any more (Genesis 26:22).

Isaac does not want to make war with the Philistines over the wells that they have clogged. Instead, he chooses to dig other wells for his herds. This passage shows us that Isaac is a man of peace, even though his son Jacob, later in the encounter with Laban, swears by the "fear of the God of Isaac" (Genesis 31:42 and 53). Now, that seems strange. How is it possible that a man of peace such as Isaac could project a terrible fear from his God?

Indeed, oral tradition tells us that Isaac was the pinnacle of might and judgment and fear. To put it simply, the angel Gabriel is with him, which is the sixth sefira from the bottom of the spiritual ladder, and the angel Michael is with Abraham, the seventh sefira from the bottom. The angel Michael is considered to be love and mercy, whereas Gabriel is judgment and the sword of God. Isaac knows that and does not want to make war against the Philistines, for he fears that the angel Gabriel will destroy them all. He prefers to avoid any confrontation by moving into another area to look for a fresh source of water for his herds. He knows that God is with him and that he will provide him with these new wells.

Isaac decides to move back to Beersheba, where he lived for some time with Abraham and knows the Well of the Seven. He also knows that the Eshel tree Abraham planted will be there. He camps that night at that spot.

Genesis 26:24 tells us that God shows himself to Isaac during the night and tells him not to be afraid, that he will be with him and bless him and his seeds for the sake of Abraham. From that point on, the angel Gabriel is with Isaac.

Isaac decides to pitch his tent at that same spot where God has shown himself to him, and then he calls in the name of God, in Genesis 26:25, as did his father, Abraham, before him.

While he is there, the servants of Isaac dig the same well Abraham has dug and calls it Beersheba (Genesis 26:33).

Now that Isaac seems to be able to find sources of water wherever he settles, King Abimelach realizes that the God of Abraham must also be with his son Isaac. To ensure that Isaac will not curse him and his people for clogging the wells, he travels to Isaac with his minister of war to sign a peace treaty with him (Genesis 26:26).

Abimelach remembers the dream after he tried to take Sarah for a wife: he was told by an angel of God that if he did not return Sarah to her husband, Abraham, who was a prophet, he and his entire household would die. This is the reason that once he realizes that Isaac has the same powers as Abraham, he decides to make peace with him as he did with his father.

In Genesis 26:28 and 29, Abimelech tells Isaac that they see that God is with Isaac, and therefore they want to make a peace treaty between them, so that they will live together in peace.

Moshe Mazin

Genesis 26:34 says that Esau, now forty years old, takes two women to be his wives. Both are Hittites, and both Isaac and Rebecca dislike them, according to Genesis 26:35.

Chapter 16   The Story of Jacob

Genesis 27:1 tells us that Isaac has become an old man whose eyes have dimmed. We know that Isaac was sixty years old when the twins were born (Genesis 25:27) and we also know that Esau and Jacob were forty when Esau took the two Hittite women as his wives. This means that Isaac was one hundred years old at the time. Still, Isaac lived to be 180 years of age. Why then does the Bible say that Isaac is getting old and his eyes have dimmed?

Earlier in Genesis 18:11, both Abraham and Sarah are described as old people when they are ninety to a hundred years of age. Indeed, when people are ninety to a hundred, they are considered old. This is why Isaac is described as an old man whose eyes are getting dim.

Genesis 27:1–2 tells us that Isaac calls Esau, his oldest son, and tells him that he does not know the date of his death, but if Esau will hunt for him that day and prepare food for him, he will bless him before he dies (Genesis 27:2–4).

Now, Rebecca knows very well that Isaac's blessing is an important one. She witnesses that when Isaac prays to God, and God grants him his wish for her to conceive. So when the time comes for Isaac to bestow his blessing upon his firstborn son, Esau, Rebecca remembers the prophecy she heard while pregnant with these twins, that the younger one would be the master of the older one. Rebecca finds Esau, the elder son, to be wild and unworthy of receiving this blessing (Genesis 25:23). That is why she intervenes and changes the course of history.

Both Esau and Jacob know that Isaac's blessing or curse will become true since God is with him. That is why Jacob is afraid to be caught in a lie to his father, according to Genesis 27:12—because the penalty will be severe if Isaac chooses to curse him.

Rebecca persuades Jacob to do what she asks of him and tells him that if his father, Isaac, curses him, it will be on her (Genesis 27:13). She prepares the kind of food that Isaac loves, and then dresses Jacob with Esau's clothing (Genesis 27:15). Because Esau is hairy (Genesis 25:25), she places goatskin over his hands and neck so that if Isaac feels Jacob's arms, he will be convinced that it is Esau.

When Jacob brings the food to Isaac, Isaac asks him who he is. Jacob answers that he is Esau (Genesis 27:19). However, Isaac is not convinced. He asks Jacob to come closer so that he can feel him (Genesis 27:21).

After feeling the hair on his hands, Isaac is still not convinced that the man standing in front of him is Esau. He asks Jacob a second time, "Is that you, my son Esau?" (Genesis 27:24), and Jacob lies again and says that it is him.

Isaac is still not convinced that he is indeed Esau after asking twice and feeling Jacob. However, he asks Jacob to give him the food and wine, and he eats and drinks it (Genesis 27:25).

After he finishes eating and drinking, he asks Jacob to come closer and to kiss him (Genesis 27:26). Obviously, Isaac uses this as an excuse to smell the clothing, to help him further identify the wearer. Then he says, "See, the fragrance of my son is like the fragrance of the field which God has blessed" (Genesis 27:27), as if he is speaking to someone other than himself and Jacob. Isaac is referring here to the Garden of Eden that God has planted.

The question here is, was there anyone else in the tent with Isaac and Jacob?

There is no clear explanation for Isaac's statement, but it is possible that he is speaking to the angel Gabriel, who is telling Isaac to check the identity of this person in detail. That is why Isaac asks Jacob several times about his identity. He further uses his senses of touch and smell to ensure the identity of that person, since he cannot see him clearly, even though he recognizes his voice as Jacob's.

It is extremely important to establish the identity of this person as Esau, because Isaac's blessing means transferring his entire capabilities to him. Also, Isaac's comparison of Esau's clothing to the smell of the Garden of Eden means Esau is endowed with the coat Adam wore when he controlled all the animals of the Earth. The Bible calls this coat of Adam's "beautiful garment," which Rebecca clothes Jacob with in Genesis 27:15.

Only after the third test is Isaac willing to give the blessing of the firstborn to Jacob, according to Genesis 27:28. It appears that Jacob lies to his father twice; his own sons will lie to him twice later in Genesis, as we shall see shortly.

As soon as Jacob leaves his father's tent, Esau enters the tent and asks his father to get up and eat from the food he has prepared, in Genesis 27:31. Now Isaac asks this new person, who are you? Esau answers that he is his oldest son, Esau (Genesis 27:33).

When Isaac hears this, he trembles in great fear, realizing that Jacob has lied to him and gotten Isaac to bless him through deceit (Genesis 27:35). However, he says to Esau, who is the one that brought me food before you came and got my blessing? blessed be he (Genesis 27:33). Isaac realizes that as hard as he tried to identify the person receiving his blessing as Esau, there was another force that decided otherwise, and therefore he accepts that decision and blesses Jacob.

When Esau asks his father for the blessing he promised him, he is told that his brother has stolen his blessing and that Isaac can't give him that same blessing.

When Esau hears his father speak like that, he cries a great cry and starts to weep, according to Genesis 27:34. Note that Esau is over forty years of age and married. For a grown man to cry in this way means that Jacob's insult and deviance is causing him great pain. No wonder he swears to himself that once Isaac is buried, he will kill his brother Jacob (Genesis 27:41).

When Isaac hears Esau's cries, he blesses him with the oil of the earth and the dew of the sky, and tells him that he will live by his sword and be a subject to his brother (Genesis 27:39–40). Indeed, today we find that most of Esau's children have oil in their land and dew on their tents or houses, which are constructed in many deserts, and that the children of Esau, being the Palestinians of today, are under the control of Israel, or Jacob's sons.

Esau's anger was so great that he must have communicated it to some of the people around him, and one of them told Rebecca of his intentions (Genesis 27:42). She realizes that Esau will indeed carry out his threat. This is why she summons Jacob and persuades him to escape to her brother Laban in Haran (Genesis 27:43).

Because both Isaac and Rebecca dislike Esau's wives, Rebecca uses this excuse to demand from Isaac that Jacob not take a wife from among the people of Canaan. Indeed, Isaac summons Jacob and tells him to take a wife from his mother's house from Haran and not from the women of Canaan (Genesis 28:1). He also proceeds to bless him by El-Shaddai, and gives him Abraham's blessings (Genesis 28:4). Abraham's blessing is the inheritance of the land of Israel that God promised him.

The Bible tells us, in Genesis 28:8 and 9, that Esau understands that Isaac dislikes the wives he took from among the Hittites, so he takes another wife from the daughters of Ishmael, the elder son of Abraham.

16.1   Jacob's ladder

Genesis 28:1 tells us that Jacob leaves Beersheba on his way to Haran. What do we know about Jacob?

So far we have encountered Jacob on two occasions. The first one was when he bought the right of the firstborn from Esau (Genesis 25:33), and the second time was when he lied to his father to get his blessings for the right of the firstborn (Genesis 27:19).

In the first encounter between Jacob and Esau, the issue of the right of the firstborn appears to be the main point of contention. These two were fighting among themselves even in Rebecca's womb, which is the reason Rebecca sought God's advice. She realized that the kind of continuous chasing of each other in her womb was not normal. Indeed, it appears that they continued to chase each other throughout their lives.

The Bible says, in Genesis 25:34, that Esau is willing to sell the rights of the firstborn for a mere dish of lentil soup and a piece of bread. He does not recognize the importance and value of the right of the firstborn, and even made fun of it.

The question that must be asked here is whether Esau should be held responsible for selling his birthright to Jacob.

A contract between two people or two entities is acknowledged as valid when something is exchanged between them. It appears that Esau received a dish of lentil soup and a loaf of bread from Jacob, which makes this contract valid and gives the right of the firstborn to Jacob. Jacob does not consider it inappropriate to receive the blessing from his father as the right of the firstborn. However, when his mother, Rebecca, asks him to deceive his father, he does object, and questions her about the lie he will be perpetrating on Isaac.

However, Rebecca convinces him that this is the right thing to do and that if there are any negative consequences, she will bear them, as discussed above.

Even so, Jacob does not escape unscathed. By directly lying to his father twice, he brings on himself later in life similar lies by his sons, according to Genesis 37:32. One cannot escape the balance of the universe.

The first lie is when he deceives Isaac into believing that he is Esau by taking advantage of the fact that Isaac's eyes are dimmed and he cannot see clearly. Later, in Genesis 29:23, Laban deceives Jacob by placing Leah in his tent at night instead of Rachel as they have agreed. This deception by Laban is done at night so that Jacob cannot see who is in his tent. As Jacob deceives Isaac by pretending to be Esau, Laban deceives Jacob by pretending that Leah, Rachel's sister, is indeed Rachel. An exact balance is struck. Two boys are balanced for two girls; and one boy is exchanged for the other and one girl is exchanged for the other.

The second lie that Jacob perpetrates on Isaac is with the garment of Esau, his brother. The lie that Jacob's sons perpetrate on him is with Joseph's garment (Genesis 37:32). Note that an exact and equal punishment is extracted from Jacob for each of his two lies. In this way, the balance between the two sides of the Tree of Life is restored. Note that the sixth sefira viewed from the top of the Tree of Life is considered to be Balance and is named after Jacob.

On the advice of his mother, Rebecca, and the command of his father, Isaac, Jacob leaves Beersheba on his way to Haran.

After one day of travel, he stumbles upon the same place where Abraham was trying to sacrifice Isaac when he was tested by God (Genesis 28:11). However, Jacob does not know that. The distance from Beersheba to the mountain of Moriah is about forty to fifty kilometers. It is important to note that Jacob intends to travel from Beersheba to Haran, which is in today's Iraq. The route that was traveled at that time was through the mountains of Judea, into the Jordan Valley, through the Golan Heights of today, through Damascus and Tadmor in today's

Syria, through Dayr Az Zawr in eastern Syria, and down into Haran. The length of this route is more than eight hundred kilometers.

It is clear that no man would attempt to walk this distance on foot, but would use a caravan or, if traveling alone, would certainly use several camels. That is why Jacob is able to travel forty to fifty kilometers in his first day. Jacob is also seeking water for his camels, which he found in the spring of today's Gihon, just below the Temple Mount of today's Temple of Solomon, as he attempted to cross the mountains of Judea.

It is also clear that once the camels drink sufficient water, and Jacob fills the leather pouches that hold water, he seeks a higher ground for camping at night. This is how he winds up at the same place where Abraham tried to sacrifice Isaac.

When Jacob reaches the top of that mountain, he notices that the sun is about to set, according to Genesis 28:11. As he prepares to spend the night, he chooses a stone for a pillow upon which to lay his head.

What happens next is a wondrous thing. Jacob sees in his dreams a ladder that extends from Earth to heaven, and many of God's angels use it to climb and descend between heaven and Earth (Genesis 28:12). Then he sees God standing over him. God tells him that he is the God of Abraham and Isaac, and that the land he is lying upon will belong to him and his descendants (Genesis 28:13). He then tells him that his seed will inherit this land and that all the nations of the earth will be blessed by him and his seed. God says he will guard him and protect him wherever he goes and that he will return him to this land to fulfill the promise he is making to him (Genesis 28:14–15).

When Jacob wakes from his sleep, he says to himself, "There must be God here." He becomes afraid and says, "How awesome is this place and I did not know; it must be the house of God, and this must be the gate to heaven" (Genesis 28:17).

The question that must be asked here is whether Jacob is talking about a portal between two levels of existence. After all, what he saw was a ladder that connected heaven and Earth.

In previous encounters between God and Abraham or Isaac, it was always a single entity, or at most three angels who appeared at such encounters. This is the first time that someone sees many angels of God using some sort of ladder or path or bridge that connects Earth and heaven. It is clear that this path has significant traffic on it, as reported by Jacob. That is why he says that it may be the gate to heaven.

Jacob's vision has been discussed by many scholars over the last several thousand years. Some of these scholars argue that Jacob's ladder represents various levels of existence.

However, in today's theoretical physics, we may call this path or bridge a wormhole in space-time.

Wormhole

(start of an article from Wikipedia)

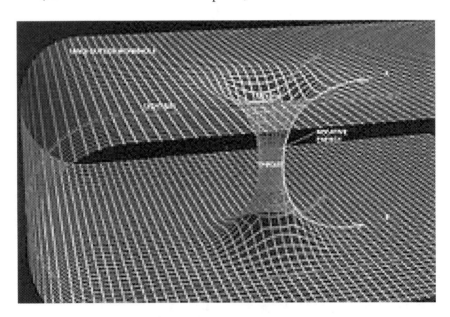

Einstein-Rosen Bridge

Analogy to a wormhole in a curved 2-D space

In physics and fiction, a **wormhole** is a hypothetical topological feature of space time that would be, fundamentally, a "shortcut" through space time. For a simple visual explanation of a wormhole, consider space time visualized as a two-dimensional (2D) surface (see illustration, above). If this surface is folded along a third dimension, it allows one to picture a wormhole "bridge." (Please note, though, that this image is merely a visualization displayed to convey an essentially *unvisualisable* structure existing in 4 or more dimensions. The parts of the wormhole could be higher-dimensional analogues for the parts of the curved 2D surface; for example, instead of mouths which are circular holes in a 2D plane, a real wormhole's mouths could be spheres in 3D space.) A wormhole is, in theory, much like a tunnel with two ends each in separate points in space time.

There is no observational evidence for wormholes, but on a theoretical level there are valid solutions to the equations of the theory of general relativity which contain wormholes. The first type of wormhole solution discovered was the **Schwarzschild wormhole** which would be present in the Schwarzschild metric describing an eternal black hole, but it was found that this type of wormhole would collapse too quickly for anything to cross from one end to the other. Wormholes which could actually be crossed, known as **traversable wormholes**, would only be possible if with negative energy density could be used to stabilize them (many physicists such as Stephen Hawking, Kip Thorne, and others believe that the Casimir effect is evidence that negative energy densities are possible in nature). Physicists have also not found any natural process which would be predicted to form a wormhole naturally in the context of general relativity, although the quantum foam hypothesis is sometimes used to suggest that tiny wormholes might appear and disappear spontaneously at the Planck scale. It has also been proposed that if a tiny wormhole held open by a negative-mass cosmic string had appeared around the time of the Big Bang, it could have been inflated to macroscopic size by cosmic inflation.

The American John Archibald Wheeler coined the term *wormhole* in 1957; however, in 1921, the German mathematician Hermann Weyl already had proposed the wormhole theory, in connection with mass analysis of electromagnetic field energy.

(end of article)

He then takes the stone that was under his head when he was sleeping, pours oil over it, and names the place the house of God or Beth El (Genesis 28:18–19).

He makes a vow that if God will be with him in this journey and provide him with food and clothing and return him safely to his home, he will contribute one-tenth of everything that God gives him to the house of God that will be built upon the rock over which he poured oil (Genesis 28:20–22). Indeed, Moses fulfills Jacob's vow by naming the house of Levi to be the priests of Israel at the house of God that Solomon built much later on the same spot. Moses orders all the remaining eleven tribes of Israel to contribute one-tenth of whatever they make to the house of God and to the Levites who serve there.

There is no clear agreement about which location is Beth El. Note that when Abraham saw God for the first time on Mount Gerizim, he named the place Beth El. The second location is here with Jacob when he names the place where he saw the ladder Beth El also.

Note that the people of Israel, after crossing the Jordan River with Joshua, have chosen Beth El on Mount Gerizim to set up the tent of the covenant, at the same place that Abraham first saw God and built an altar.

This new Beth El, or the house of God that Jacob has named, is where the Temple of Solomon was later built. Both places are holy, but the one in Jerusalem of today is the final choice for the house of God.

16.2   Jacob's tribulation in Haran

Genesis 29:2 tells us that when Jacob finally arrives at Haran, he encounters a well of water with three herds of sheep waiting to drink from it. It turns out that the well has a large stone over it, and only when all the herds and the herdsman are present at the same time can the stone be removed (Genesis 29:3). The reason for the large stone that required many men to remove was exactly so that no specific herd would drink from the well before the others.

Jacob asks the herdsman present about Laban. He finds out that he is well known, and that his daughter Rachel is just coming to the well with her herd (Genesis 29:6). He then asks the herdsman why they are not letting the herds drink from the well. The herdsmen tell him that they cannot remove the stone (because of its size and weight) unless all the other men with their herds are present so that they can remove the stone together and all the herds can drink from the well at the same time (Genesis 29:8).

As he sees Rachel coming to the well with her herd, he decides to remove the stone alone so that Rachel's herd will be able to drink (Genesis 29:10). This act of Jacob tells us that he was a mighty man and that he also wanted to impress Rachel. He also thought that the day was still young and that the herds should not wait until the end of the day, when all the herds returned from the fields, to satisfy their thirst. This shows that Jacob was a caring man.

After doing this, he gives water to Rachel's herd and proceeds to kiss her and identify himself. This act of kissing a friend or family member is still done to this day in the Middle East. However, as he identifies himself to Rachel, he bursts out crying, according to Genesis 29:11.

Why did Jacob cry?

Let us consider this issue. Jacob was not a man of the field; as the Bible puts it, "he was a dweller of the tents" (Genesis 25:27), meaning that he preferred civilized settings and did not venture into the fields that frequently.

This time he was ordered by his mother and father to travel to Haran, a distance of more than eight hundred kilometers, all alone. It must have been several weeks before Jacob reached Haran. Being alone for so long and finally seeing a member of his family must have caused him to be very emotional, and that is why he cries.

As soon as he tells Rachel who he is, she runs to her father's house and tells him about Jacob (Genesis 29:12). Laban comes out to meet Jacob and invites him into his home. He then tells Jacob that he is flesh of his flesh and should stay with them for at least a month (Genesis 29:14).

16.2.1   Jacob's stay at Laban's house

Over this first month, Jacob helps Laban with all kinds of tasks in the field in order to be polite and to earn his stay. Laban then tells Jacob that because he is family, he should not work for him for nothing. He asks him what his pay should be (Genesis 29:15).

The Bible tells us that Laban has two daughters: the older one is Leah, and the younger one is Rachel (Genesis 29:16). We learn in the next verse that Jacob loves Rachel, for she is beautiful, both in her face and her body (Genesis 29:17). This is understandable since Jacob notices Rachel from the first moment he sees her at the well, and being with Laban for one month only intensifies those feelings, whereas her older sister, Leah, on the other hand, has "tender eyes." In today's medical terms, we would call Leah's condition lazy eye syndrome.

Jacob tells his uncle that he will work for him for seven years in order to pay for Rachel to be his wife (Genesis 29:18). Laban agrees to the offer and says that it is better to give Rachel to him than to a stranger (Genesis 29:19).

The Bible says that these seven years seemed like a few days to Jacob, because he was happy and eager to be with Rachel as husband and wife (Genesis 29:20). These seven years will later be the seven good years that Joseph foresaw in Pharaoh's dream. The seven years come to an end, and Jacob asks Laban to give him Rachel as he promised (Genesis 29:21). Laban makes a great feast for the local community and then brings Leah to Jacob's tent during the night, according to Genesis 29:23. The next morning, Jacob discovers that it was Leah he was with all night and not Rachel (Genesis 29:25). He then asks Laban, "Why have you done this to me? It was Rachel that I worked for; why did you deceive me?" (Genesis 29:25).

Laban answers that it is a tradition in this community that a younger woman cannot be given for marriage before her older sister (Genesis 29:26). Indeed, Laban's statement is correct for the people of the Middle East; however, he could have told Jacob that at the start of the seven years rather than at the conclusion. It is clear that Laban intentionally deceived Jacob. I explained the reason for this deception in terms of the balance earlier, even though Jacob and Laban were not aware of it.

However, Laban tells him that if he works for him another seven years, he will also give him Rachel for a wife (Genesis 29:27). Note that the second set of seven years is proposed by Laban and not Jacob. Jacob considers them the "bad" seven years that Joseph later foresees in Pharaoh's dream.

Jacob obliges and does as Laban says, according to Genesis 29:28. Note that Laban gives each of his daughters her own maid, Zilpah for Leah and Bilhah for Rachel. These two maids will later be Jacob's concubines. After the second set of seven years passes, Laban gives Rachel to Jacob as his wife (Genesis 29:28).

Now, because Jacob loves Rachel very much, he naturally spends most of his time with her. However, God gives Leah a son as compensation for her suffering, and she names him Reuben, which in Hebrew means "See, it is a boy" (Genesis 29:32). God gives Leah another son, whom she names Simon. She says that God has heard her plea, and therefore she names him Simon, which in Hebrew has the root of the verb "to hear" (Genesis 29:33).

Leah names her third son Levi, (ל ו י), which in Hebrew means "he is for God" (Genesis 29:34). However, her intention in naming this boy Levi is that now that she has borne three boys of Jacob's, she thinks that he will surely be her companion (י ל ו ה). Indeed, Moses fulfills Leah's prophecy and names the tribe of Levi as the priests of Israel.

When Leah's fourth son is born, she names him Judah; she does this as thanks to God (Genesis 29:35). However, in Hebrew, the name of Judah is spelled י ה ו ד ה, *yod, hah, vav, dalet,* and *hah*. Note that the fourth letter in Judah's name is *dalet,* which is also the first letter of King David's name. If one removes the *dalet,* the remaining word is *Yahweh,* which is the name of God.

Once Leah delivers Judah, she stops conceiving (Genesis 29:35).

The Bible tells us that Rachel is jealous of her sister Leah for having children, whereas she is unable to do so. According to Genesis 30:1, she threatens Jacob with suicide if he does not give her children. However, Jacob becomes angry with her and says, "Am I God who prevented you from having children?" (Genesis 30:2).

This is indeed a curious thing. After all, Rachel and Leah are sisters: if Leah can deliver four children, why can't Rachel conceive at all?

We do not know the answer to this question. However, it is possible that a balance was struck between Jacob and Rachel's love and Leah's children. Rachel has Jacob's love and most of his time, whereas Leah has to be satisfied with her children.

Rachel is not ready to give up, and she asks Jacob to sleep with her maid Bilhah so that she may conceive through her (Genesis 30:3). Indeed, Jacob sleeps with Bilhah, and she conceives and delivers a baby boy. Because Bilhah is Rachel's maid, she is considered her property;

therefore, Rachel is the one who names this boy, and she names him Dan, which in Hebrew means "judgment" (Genesis 30:6).

Now that Bilhah has become one of Jacob's concubines, he continues to visit her, and she conceives again. This time Rachel names him Naphtali, which in Hebrew means "schemes" (Genesis 30:8).

Now that Leah has stopped conceiving, she takes her maid Zilpah and gives her to Jacob to produce more children. Indeed, Zilpah delivers two boys. Leah names the first one Gad. It is not clear what this name means. The second one she names Asher, which means "happiness" (Genesis 30:10–13).

It is clear that both Rachel and Leah are battling over Jacob's affection and love. It seems that these two sisters decide to battle it out by bringing as many children to Jacob as possible. That is why both of them resort even to the legal usage of their maids as a mean to an end, resulting in delivering more children to Jacob.

The Bible tells us that on one occasion, when Reuben is in the field in the days of the harvest, he finds a fruit called Dudaim, which some scholars suggest had the power of fertility (Genesis 30:14). Indeed, Rachel must think so, since she asks Leah to give her some of the fruit, possibly to help her get pregnant (Genesis 30:14). Leah answers her by saying in the next verse, "Is it not enough that you have taken my man—now you also want this fruit that my son brought for me?"

Rachel must have recognized the power of this fruit, because she agrees to have Jacob spend the night with Leah. Indeed, when Jacob returns from the field, Leah informs him that a bargain was struck between her and Rachel and that he will spend the night with her (Genesis 30:16).

After this event, Leah conceives and delivers a baby boy, whom she names Issachar, meaning "reward" (Genesis 30:18).

She conceives again and delivers a sixth boy, whom she names Zebulun, meaning "endowment" (Genesis 30:20). Then she conceives again and delivers a girl, whom she names Dinah, which is the female version of "judgment" (Genesis 30:21). Leah does this to counter Rachel's claims of judgment with the name of Dan.

Oral tradition tells us that Leah's six boys and one girl stand for the six days of creation and the Sabbath, considered the domain of the Holy Spirit, which has a female aspect (Zohar).

It seems that when this event is fulfilled, Rachel is allowed to conceive. Indeed, she gives birth to a baby boy whom she names Joseph, meaning "may God add more children to me" (Genesis 30:24).

16.3 Jacob's return to Canaan

Now that Rachel has delivered Joseph, Jacob asks Laban to let him return to his land (Genesis 30:25). He says to Laban, "Give me my wives and my children and I will leave." However, Laban tells Jacob that he consulted his "gods," which Genesis 30:27 says are sacrilegious idols of black magic, with the snake being the main deity, and was told that Yahweh has blessed him with wealth because of Jacob.

Laban is known to be a master of black magic, which he uses frequently. By consulting his gods, he has learned that his wealth is attributable mainly to Jacob's presence with him since the God of Jacob favored him and blessed him and all those around him benefited from the blessings. In short, Laban did not want to lose Jacob's presence and the blessing of his God, for his wealth might diminish.

Let us examine this in more depth.

As I stated earlier, the worship of evil was common in Mesopotamia and in the ancient world, based on the evolved being that was banished from the Garden of Eden along with Adam and Eve. That deity was called Baal, or, as we know him today, Satan.

It is clear therefore that the people of the region were skilled in the art of black magic. It appears that Laban was a master of it. Among the so-called "Teraphim" (Genesis 31:34), or idols that Laban possesses and whom he considers his gods (Genesis 31:30), is an idol of a snake.

When Laban speaks to Jacob about the consultation with his gods, he tells him that he consulted the snake and learned that his wealth was caused by Jacob's presence in his house.

We also know that Rachel is very much aware of her father's usage of black magic and the snake idols. That is why she steals these idols and hides them beneath her as she rides on the camel (Genesis 31:34). She does not mention any of this to Jacob because she knows he will be very angry, since he knows these idols are sacrilegious.

When Laban explains to Jacob how he came to understand Jacob's presence with him and that he would like him to continue to stay with him, Jacob does not respond but is quiet.

When Laban sees that Jacob is quiet, he asks him to name his price (Genesis 30:28). Jacob says to Laban that he is well aware that when he joined his household, Laban had only a few herds. Since that time God has increased his wealth because of Jacob, and now Jacob would like to increase his wealth too (Genesis 30:29–30).

To that answer Laban asks, "What can I give you?"

Jacob says, "Don't give me anything, but if you do this for me, I will stay and be a shepherd to your herds." He then tells Laban that all the sheep and goats that have spots on them will be his, and those of solid color will be Laban's (Genesis 30:32).

Laban agrees to this proposal. However, he assembles his sons and tells them to round up all the sheep and goats that have spots on them and keep them away at a distance of three days (Genesis 30:35–36). He then leaves the solid-colored animals with Jacob.

Jacob now has a clear message: that Laban has no intention of giving him anything at all. He then takes fresh rods of poplar and hazel and chestnut, peels white streaks in them, and places them in the watering receptacles to which the flocks come to drink (Genesis 30:37-38).

When the flocks drink from the water, they all conceive and give birth to spotted sheep and goats, and he gives any solid-color animals to Laban, according to Genesis 30:39. He then took all the newborn spotted flocks and separated them from Laban's herds.

In this way, Jacob's wealth increases tremendously and he purchases slaves, both male and female, camels, and donkeys.

16.3.1   Laban's contest with Jacob

Genesis 31:1 says that Jacob heard the sons of Laban saying that Jacob had taken all the wealth from their father, and that he made his wealth from their father. Indeed, the next verse says Jacob noticed that Laban was no longer friendly with him.

At this point, God tells Jacob to return to his home and to his father's house, and that he will be with him (Genesis 31:3).

Before making that decision, Jacob consults with both Leah and Rachel. He tells them that Laban, their father, is no longer friendly with him, and that the God of his father has told him to return home. He then tells them that their father tried to deceive him by reducing or changing his pay ten times, but that God did not allow that to happen (Genesis 31:4–7).

He tells his wives that their father has changed his agreement about the type of flocks that may belong to Jacob ten times. When he said the spotted flocks would be Jacob's, indeed it was so, and when he changed his mind again and said that only the solid-color flocks would belong to Jacob, God has caused this to be so (Genesis 31:8). He further tells them that an angel of God showed himself to him in a dream and told him to return to his land.

Both Rachel and Leah answer Jacob and tell him that because their father sold them and "ate" the money of the sale, which in this case was fourteen years of Jacob's labor, all the wealth that Jacob has made is for them and their children (Genesis 31:14–16). Furthermore, they tell him to go ahead and do exactly as God has commanded him.

The phrase "eat the money" is still commonly used today among the Jewish people of Baghdad, Iraq, who immigrated to Israel. It means that he spent the money.

After this event, and after receiving permission from both Rachel and Leah, Jacob assembles all his herds and all his wealth in order to return to Canaan. He uses the occasion when Laban and his sons leave to shear the sheep to implement his escape plan, according to Genesis 31:19.

Just to make sure that their father, Laban, will not use black magic to harm them, Rachel steals his sacrilegious idols (Genesis 31:19).

Now Jacob has run away without telling Laban that he is leaving, causing Laban to be very angry. Furthermore, he is furious about the theft of the sacrilegious idols (Genesis 31:20).

Jacob crosses the Euphrates River on his way to Canaan. Three days later, Laban is told that Jacob has escaped (Genesis 31:22). Laban assembles all his sons, who are Jacob's brothers-in-law, as the Bible indicates, and his own brothers, and chases Jacob's party for seven days, until he catches up with him (Genesis 31:23).

The night before Laban actually reaches Jacob, God appears to him in a dream and tells him to be careful in speaking with Jacob, whether what he has to say is good or bad (Genesis 31:24). In other words, Laban is warned against troubling Jacob at all. Indeed, when he reaches the site of Jacob's camp, he leaves Jacob's brothers-in-law at some distance while he alone continues to speak with Jacob.

He then asks Jacob why he deceived him by running away and why he has taken his daughters with him as if they were captives of the sword (Genesis 31:26). Laban says that if Jacob had let him know that he intended to leave, he would have sent him with gladness and with songs and timbrel and lyre (Genesis 31:27).

Now he tells Jacob that what Jacob did was stupid—escaping without letting him kiss his daughters and grandchildren. Laban continues and says he has the means to harm Jacob (Genesis 31:29); however, he tells him that the God of Jacob's father told him the previous night to be careful in speaking with Jacob, either good or bad.

Laban then says (verse 30) that he understands that Jacob missed his father's house, but why steal Laban's gods?

Jacobs answers that he was afraid Laban would take his daughters away from him; as for Laban's gods, he says that whoever took them will not live. Furthermore, he tells Laban to search the camp and take whatever belongs to him (Genesis 31:31–32).

When Jacob says that whoever stole Laban's gods will not live, he does not know that Rachel is the one who stole her father's sacrilegious idols. As far as Jacob is concerned, anyone who possesses these sacrilegious idols should not live. It is clear to him that these idols are evil.

Laban searches all the tents in the camp and finds nothing. The Bible tells us, in Genesis 31:35, that he literally felt every inch of every tent with his hands while searching for the idols.

Now that Jacob sees how Laban searches the tents with such extreme care, he gets angry. It suggests that Jacob has stolen many things from Laban, and he knows this is not the case at all. It is like saying Jacob and his household are known thieves (Genesis 31:36).

According to Genesis 31:37, he then asks Laban, "What is my crime that you have chased me all this way and gone into all my tents and felt every item by hand? What have you found? Indeed, put whatever item you have found that belongs to you in front of my brethren and your brothers so that they will be able to judge us both.

"After all, I've been with you for twenty years, and not one sheep or goat was missing from your herds. I've guarded your herds in the heat of the summer [the Iraqi summer is very oppressive, with temperatures reaching to 50°C or 125°F] and the cold nights of winter. I worked for you for fourteen years for both of your daughters, and another six years herding your herds, and you have changed my pay ten times. If it was not for the God of my fathers, the God of Abraham, and the fear of

Isaac, you would have sent me without anything, but God has seen this and warned you last night about this issue" (Genesis 31:38–42).

It appears that Jacob is finally speaking about his anger at Laban's deceit over this twenty-year period of time. Remember, Laban is Jacob's uncle, and there was a degree of respect as a result of that.

Laban answers Jacob, saying, "The daughters are mine, and their children are mine; now, what can I do to them or to their children?" By that he meant that he could do no harm to them or to their children. Therefore, he proposed to Jacob that they establish a peace treaty between the two of them, and that this peace treaty be witness between them both (Genesis 31:44).

This is agreeable to Jacob, and he takes a stone from around him and lifts it up as a symbol of a monument. He asks his brethren to join him in setting up the monument made up of stones. After setting it up, they celebrate the event by eating food together, according to Genesis 31:46.

The next verse says Laban named that place "Ya'gar Shahadota," which in Aramaic means "witnessing mound," and Jacob named it "Galeed," which means "witnessing monument" in Hebrew. Laban then tells Jacob that the monument will be a witness between both of them after they are out of sight of each other. He has Jacob swear not to ill-treat his daughters and not to take any other wife over them. He tells him that no one but God can see to these things, and therefore God will be a witness between them (Genesis 31:48–52).

Laban then swears to Jacob by the gods of Abraham and by his own grandfather Nachor to seal this agreement, and Jacob swears by the fears of his father, Isaac (Genesis 31:53). After this event, Jacob calls for his brethren to break bread with him and Laban.

The fact that both are willing to share bread and food with each other means that the agreement is accepted by both parties. This was the ancient way of concluding a treaty. To some degree it is still the custom in the Middle East.

On the morning of the next day, Laban kisses his daughters and grandchildren and blesses them, and then returns to Haran while Jacob continues on his way.

16.4 Jacob is challenged by an angel

After leaving Gilead, Jacob continues toward the passage of the Yabbok River, which is on the east side of the Jordan River. The Yabbok River spills into the Jordan River at just about the same latitude as the city of Shecem, which today is Nablus in the West Bank of Israel.

Genesis 32:23 tells us that as Jacob continued his way toward the Yabbok River passage, a group of angels bumps into him. When Jacob sees them, he says they are a camp of God, and he calls the place Mahanaim, meaning "two camps."

This is strange indeed. Why would Jacob call the place a camp of two?

Let us examine this.

Jacob is getting closer to the land of Canaan, where his destiny will unfold. He has just escaped from Laban, who intended to harm him and his entire party. He was able to overcome the obstacles Laban placed in his path for nearly twenty years, even though Laban was a master of black magic.

It is clear that before Jacob is allowed to enter the land of Canaan, he will be challenged again and by Satan himself. It is not likely that the being called Satan will allow Jacob entrance into the land that was promised to him by God without being challenged. It is not in Satan's interest to allow Jacob an entrance into Canaan, for he will flourish there and fulfill his destiny. Also, God has showed himself to all three patriarchs only in that land and nowhere else. It means that the land of Canaan is holy ground, and that if Jacob enters it, his spiritual powers will grow since he will be in the vicinity of God. Satan does not like any of these possibilities.

The reason Jacob is challenged and nobody else is that he is the carrier of the covenant between God and the people of Israel.

It appears that Satan has used Laban to hold and delay Jacob's return to his father's land for a period of twenty years, until Jacob gains such power, including mastering the black arts, that Laban cannot stop him any longer. Mastering the black arts does not mean that one has to use them. This is a natural fallout when one obtains knowledge, since knowledge has two sides. By knowing the side of creation as Jacob does now, he also knows the destructive power of knowledge, the so-called black art.

Laban knows Jacob's power has exceeded his after Jacob is able to cause the herds to deliver spotted offspring. When Laban changes that decree to solid-color herds, Jacob's power causes the herds again to deliver exactly what he wants, against the wishes of Laban, as was stated earlier.

When Satan declares a challenge of this magnitude against Jacob, it is well known among the angels in heaven. This is why this group of angels decides to inform Jacob about this challenge. Indeed, they go out looking for him and bump against him near the Yabbok River.

As Jacob reaches the passage of the Yabbok River, he sends messengers to his brother, Esau, and commands them to say to his "master," Esau (Genesis 32:5–6), "I have lived with Laban and been delayed until now. I have acquired oxen, donkeys, flocks, servants, and maidservants, and I have sent word to you so that I will find favor in your eyes."

Jacob's message to Esau is very strange. Why would he inflate his brother's fury even more by claiming to have wealth of all kinds? Is it not the last thing his brother wants to hear?

To understand this message, one must understand the brothers' relationship. The Bible tells us that Esau was a hunter and a man of the field; he was used to dealing with all kinds of animals, from camels to horses and goats and sheep.

Jacob, on the other hand, is a tent dweller who rarely if ever ventures into the field. Therefore, he sends this message to demonstrate to his brother that he too has become a man of the field, much like his brother Esau.

The message is meant to convey that they are now alike, and only Esau would understand its meaning.

However, when the messengers come back, they tell him Esau is coming toward him with a crowd of four hundred men (Genesis 32:7). The meaning of the number four hundred is explained earlier when Abraham buys the cave of Machpelah from the Hittites.

Note that these four hundred men were with Satan the night he fought with Jacob and was defeated. After this defeat, all four hundred angels with Satan join Esau as men for the final battle to kill Jacob and all who are with him. This is the second camp that Jacob has seen, and where he named the place Mahaniam, according to Genesis 32:7.

This causes Jacob to fear greatly (Genesis 32:8), because he thinks the fact that his brother is coming with such a crowd can only mean that he intends to kill Jacob and all those with him. After all, if Esau was coming in peace, he does not need a crowd of four hundred men. To that end, Jacob divides his party into two camps, one camp with Leah and her maid and their children, and the other camp with Rachel and her maid and their children. Jacob says to himself that if one camp is stricken, at least the other one will survive (Genesis 32: 8–9).

During that night, Jacob orders his servants to take many herds of all kinds of animals as a gift to his brother Esau, for he thinks such a gift may temper his anger (Genesis 32:21). He orders his servants to follow each other with their herds with some distance between so that Esau will clearly see the various herds offered to him. He further orders his servants to tell Esau that all these herds are gifts from Jacob and that each one of them should say that Jacob follows behind.

That same night, Jacob rises up and goes over the passage of the Yabbok River with all his wives, their children, and all his herds and many servants (Genesis 32:24). Once he gets them all across the river, he stays behind, knowing he will be challenged by Satan.

Genesis 32:25 tells us that a "man" wrestles with Jacob all night, and at sunrise, seeing that he cannot defeat Jacob, he asks to let him leave. However, Jacob refuses to set him free and asks him for his blessing (Genesis 32:27).

In return, this "man" asks Jacob for his name, and when Jacob tells him his name is Jacob, the "man" says his name will no longer be Jacob but Israel. He explains that his name is Israel because of the fact that he wrestled with a divine being and with men and was not defeated (Genesis 32:28).

He then is forced to bless Jacob (Genesis 32:29).

The first question is why Jacob would transfer his wives, children, and all his belongings during the night. After all, it would have been much easier and much safer to cross the Yabbok River during the day. Furthermore, he is now on the same side as Esau and his men without the benefit of the river as a divider and shield.

The answer is that Jacob knows that he will be challenged that same night at the northern bank of the river, and he wants to make sure none of his family members or any of his servants and living animals with him will be harmed. He knows that in a battle zone, innocent people or other living things can be harmed. He basically wants to clear the area of everyone so that Satan cannot harm them.

The fact that he transfers everyone across the Yabbok River during the night indicates that Satan, who controls the first shift of the night (early evening until midnight), recognizes that Jacob is clearing the area for them to do battle. Indeed, he allows him to do so since he sees that Jacob does not intend to escape the battle.

The second issue, wrestling with an angel, is very odd. How can Jacob, who is a man, wrestle with an angel, let alone defeat him and hold him captive all night? Furthermore, why would Jacob ask for a blessing from an evil being, and why ask for this being's name (Genesis 32:28)?

The answer to the first question is this: Jacob has the blessing of his father, Isaac, with him and his spiritual power. This blessing contains both the power of love and the power of might. This means that Jacob controlls both sides of the Tree of Knowledge, which gives him the upper hand over this angel or advanced being who was banished from Eden.

One can think of this as being master of light and dark. This is why he is able to have Satan as a captive all night. Indeed, the fact that this wrestling takes place during the night indicates the presence of negative forces. As was said in Genesis, God sees the "light to be good and he called it day," which indicates that night is not necessarily good.

We know that all living things require light to grow and flourish, whereas if they lack light they will die. Furthermore, this angel does not wish to struggle with Jacob during the day but only at night. Indeed, he is afraid of the light, as was said in Genesis 32:27.

The ability to defeat Satan is clear, given that Jacob possesses the mastery of darkness along with the light, and that he also is familiar with all the black magic his uncle Laban did.

These twenty years with Laban have taught Jacob all the secrets of black magic, not that he needs them, but by knowing them he is able to defeat the wishes of both Laban and Satan. Furthermore, we know that this "man" is indeed an angel, for he says so when he tells Jacob that he wrestled with man and with "Elohim" (א ל ה י ם) and won, in Genesis 32:30. The word *Elohim* means an "angel of God" or an advanced being, as was stated in chapter 10.2.

The next question is why he asks Satan to bless him.

The answer to this question is this: Jacob asks Satan to bless him because he knows that such a blessing requires the admission that God is the king of the universe and that he is God. In any Hebrew blessing, such as the blessing of the fruit of the earth, one says, "Blessed art thou the Lord our God, king of the universe, who has brought fruit from the earth."

This means that Jacob has forced Satan to admit that God is his God and he is the king of the universe.

When Satan is forced to utter these words, he becomes very angry and kicks Jacob on his left thigh (Genesis 32:26), which has made the thigh of any animal sacrilegious to the Jewish people to this day. Note that during the entire night there is no physical battle, only spiritual. However, when it is clear that Jacob is holding the angel captive and will not release him even though he asks to be released, the angel resorts to physical contact in order to be released.

How is it possible that Satan does not know who he is wrestling with, since he asks Jacob for his name in Genesis 32:28?

One explanation is that in order to bless a person, one needs to know his name. It is possible that Jacob was known by another name that was associated with his soul and that Satan did not know his earthly name.

Another question is why Jacob would want to know the name of this being.

Indeed, the Bible never mentions the being's name. We refer to him as Satan, which means the one who "derailed" the path of mankind globally, and the paths of man and woman in particular.

By knowing his name, one could identify him without him being able to hide. This could give the upper hand to mankind in dealing with hidden and creeping evil without the knowledge of the people being acted on—much like a snake in the grass that cannot be heard before it strikes. This is the reason Jacob asked for his name.

After the battle with Satan, Jacob names the place Peniel, which means "the face of God." Indeed, Jacob recognizes that this "man" was a divine being, according to Genesis 32:31.

Note here that even though this angel tells Jacob his new name, Israel, the Bible does not use Israel until Jacob sees God again in Beth El, when he identifies himself as "El-Shaddai" and reconfirms Jacob's new name. This means Jacob has some doubt in his mind about the new name given to him by the angel with whom he wrestled.

Jacob then crosses the Yabbok River, limping to join his party, and the entire party continues toward the plain of the Jordan River.

16.5 Jacob meets his brother, Esau

Genesis 33:1 tells us that Jacob sees his brother, Esau, with four hundred men and immediately divides the party into the two camps he organized earlier. As mentioned before, Jacob is afraid Esau is going to kill all of them, and in this way, he hopes that if Esau strikes one camp, the other will survive (Genesis 32:9). Once he does this, he moves forward to be in front of his entire party (Genesis 33:3).

It is clear to Jacob that Esau is very angry and intends to kill Jacob and all who are with him. As we said earlier, if Esau wants to meet Jacob for a peaceful purpose, he does not need so many men. Note that Laban came with only a few men, and he still knew he could harm Jacob and all of his. Therefore, Esau does indeed intend to kill Jacob and all who are with him. His anger is so great that even after twenty years since the stealing of the birthright of the firstborn, his anger has not abated. Obviously, Rebecca was wrong in assuming that Esau's anger would subside after a few days (Genesis 27:44).

Jacob knows that Esau coming with four hundred men means he is going to kill him and all of his. However, he also knows that God promised him to be with him and protect him (Genesis 31:3), and he is correct. Because God intervened on his behalf with Laban, he is not afraid of Esau or his small army.

The other reason for this confidence is his knowledge that he controls spiritual powers far stronger than any army of Esau. We found that Jacob wrestled with an angel of God and was able to hold him captive with his spiritual powers (Genesis 32:27).

Note that Jacob approaches Esau by bowing to him seven times (Genesis 33:3). When Esau sees this, he runs to his brother, Jacob, and embraces and kisses him, and they both cry together.

The Bible does not explain why Jacob bows to Esau seven times, no more and no less.

Jacob has not given up on his brother Esau since they were in their mother's womb; he certainly is not going to give up on him now. This is why Jacob held on to Esau's ankle while they were in their mother's womb, and the act of the seven bows now is meant to bring Esau into the fold of God's light.

Even though Esau thinks Jacob is bowing to him, in fact, Jacob is bowing once to each of the seven divine levels of the Tree of Life, as Abraham did when El-Shaddai showed himself to him (Genesis 17:3).

Esau doesn't realize that each of these bows has caused him to be elevated to a higher sefira, or dimension, until they reach the seventh sefira, which is the sefira of love and compassion. In effect, Jacob is holding Esau as he did at birth as he climbs with him to the seventh sefira. We witness the spiritual power of Jacob when he wrestles with the angel and the angel cannot release himself from Jacob's spiritual grip before crossing the Yabbok River. Jacob has used the same spiritual power to hold Esau and to elevate him to the sefira of love and compassion.

One can understand the effect of these elevations by considering seven concentric circles, where the final circle is a point. Jacob starts from the seventh circle, and his spiritual energy is constantly being focused on smaller and smaller circles. Therefore, by the time he reaches Esau, his entire spiritual energy is focused on him. Jacob's spiritual energy is so strong that it causes any darkness within Esau to retreat. The actual bows that Jacob performs are meant to ease Esau's mind, and at the same time appeal to higher divine power and assure Esau that Jacob still considers him his older brother and "master," as he tells the messengers he sends to Esau in Genesis 32:5.

This spiritual hold on Esau demonstrates itself later when he decides to move out of Canaan into Edom (Genesis 36:6), where it says that Esau left the land of Canaan because of Jacob his brother. The explanation given in the Bible is that the land could not support both of them because of their wealth. However, why should Esau leave the land just to please Jacob? It seems that Jacob is the newcomer, not Esau, and that if anyone were to leave, it should be Jacob. The Bible clearly says that Esau moves to a new land because of his brother's face, which in biblical culture means that something powerful has caused him to leave (Genesis 36:6).

When Esau is cleansed in this way and has the light of God shining through him, he understands love, mercy, and compassion. Oral tradition tells us that only his head was allowed to be buried in the cave of Machpelah, but not his body, which he had contaminated with the women of Canaan.

After this event, Jacob introduces his wives and their children to Esau, and each one in turn bows to Jacob's older brother. Jacob then offers all the gifts of herds that he sent ahead of him, but Esau tells him he has plenty and does not need any of Jacob's herds.

After much insistence by Jacob, Esau agrees to accept the gifts (Genesis 33:11).

Now Esau suggests to Jacob that he travel with him to wherever Jacob is going. However, Jacob tells his brother that with so many young children and newborn herds, it will be difficult for him to keep pace with his brother and his party. He tells Esau that it is better for his brother to go on while he makes his way at a slower pace (Genesis 33:14).

Esau understands Jacob's argument, bids him farewell, and returns to the land of Edom while Jacob continues toward the junction of the Yabbok and Jordan Rivers (Genesis 33:16–17).

Indeed, the Bible tells us that he travels to a place called Succoth, which in Hebrew means "houses of reeds." Note that reeds could be found at the junction of these two rivers, and that is where Jacob decided to settle down, according to Genesis 33:17.

Chapter 17   The Story of Dinah

Once Jacob has settled there, he travels to Shechem, the capital of the region, to buy the land from its legal owner. The entire area is controlled by the lord of Shechem, and Jacob buys the land from him for a hundred pieces of uncontested currency, according to Genesis 33:19. There is no clear understanding of this currency; however, it must have been either gold or silver, which was acceptable anywhere in the Middle East.

The Bible tells us, in Genesis 33:18, that Jacob came into the city of Shechem intact. Indeed, that was the promise that Jacob made to God as he was departing Canaan for the city of Haran. Now that he has returned intact and physically unharmed, and with wealth, wives, and children, it is time to acknowledge God's guidance. Therefore, Jacob builds an altar and proclaims that God is the God of Israel, as he vowed to do at the site of the gate of heaven (Genesis 33:20).

Oral tradition tells us that the land that Jacob buys from the lord of the city of Shechem is the place where Joseph is buried later (Zohar) as part of the land of the tribe of Ephraim.

Now that Jacob has legally purchased the land, he builds a house for himself and his household, and builds houses of reeds for his flocks and herds, according to Genesis 33:17.

Genesis 34:1 tells us that Dinah, the daughter of Leah, is curious about the local girls and goes out from the safety of her home to observe their customs. This curiosity costs her dearly.

At this point, Dinah is no more than ten or twelve years old. We know this from the following: Leah started having children in her first year as Jacob's wife. Considering a natural distance between children of approximately a year and a half to two years means that the first four boys were born in the first six to eight years. Thereafter, Leah was not able to have more children for nearly three or four years. After this, she delivered two more boys, which means another three to four years have passed. Only then did she deliver her daughter, Dinah.

If we consider the lower time range, we are looking at twelve years before Dinah is conceived and comes into the world. We also know that Jacob stayed with Laban for twenty years; this means that by the time Jacob reaches Succoth, Dinah is little more than ten to twelve years old, which makes her a child and not even a teenager. Indeed, the prince of the land calls her a child when he asks his father to beg Jacob to give her to him as a wife (Genesis 34:4).

As it turns out, the prince of the land, known as Shechem Ben Hamor the Hivvite, finds her to be very attractive and rapes and tortures her, according to Genesis 34:2.

The word *Hivvite* in Aramaic means "serpentine." The Bible is hinting that this prince of Shechem was evil and like a snake in his character.

It appears that the prince enjoys his sadistic torture of Dinah, for he asks his father to take the girl as a wife for him.

When Jacob finds out from the other girls who were with her at the time of the kidnapping that his daughter was raped and tortured by the prince of the city, he remains quiet until his children return home from the fields (Genesis 34:5).

It is clear that the girls could not stop the prince from forcing himself on Dinah. Furthermore, after he fulfills his desires, he takes Dinah with him to his house. Is it any wonder that the sons of Jacob are furious? Not only has this man raped their sister but he is still holding her captive in his house. When they hear what has happened to their sister, Dinah, they become angry and sad at the same time, according to Genesis 34:7.

Realizing that his son, Shechem, has committed a serious crime against Jacob and his family, the lord of the city of Shechem hurries up toward Jacob to speak with him and resolve the matter (Genesis 34:6).

He tells Jacob and his children that his son the prince desires Jacob's daughter for a wife, and to ease the tension over her rape and torture, he offers a resolution that would allow Jacob's family to wed the daughters of Shechem and vice versa (Genesis 34:8–9).

Jacob's elder sons, Reuben, Simon, and Levi, take the lead in responding to the lord of Shechem.

The Bible tells us that when they answer Hamor, they are not speaking the truth (Genesis 34:13). Indeed, they intend to deceive Hamor. Here we find that the Bible is looking at the intention behind the words and not at the words only, because if we examine what they are saying to Hamor, we see that they are indeed speaking the truth in regard to wedding anyone who is not circumcised (Genesis 34:14).

They say they cannot give their sister as a wife to a man who is not circumcised, since this is sacrilege to them. However, if the people of Shechem will accept circumcision of all males, then giving their sister to the son of Hamor will be acceptable to them and they will be willing to wed each other's daughters and become one nation (Genesis 34:15–16).

However, if the people of Shechem do not accept circumcision, they will take their sister and leave (Genesis 34:17).

Note that during this conversation, Dinah is still held captive at the house of Shechem, the son of Hamor.

Is it any wonder that Jacob's sons intend to deceive Hamor? It is not clear to them how else they will get their sister back. Furthermore, what they say to Hamor is indeed true, and in regard to their statement, they are not lying. However, what follows is what infuriates Jacob.

Now that Hamor has his answer, he has to persuade the people of his city to accept the proposal that Jacob's sons put forward. To do this, he and his son assemble all the people of the city at the city gate and explain the proposal in detail (Genesis 34:20). However, in order to make sure that the proposal is accepted by the people, Hamor suggests to them that Jacob and his sons' great wealth will become theirs once the two groups have intermarried (Genesis 34:23).

Indeed, the people of Shechem like this proposal very much, since it seems they will greatly benefit from it. They accept Hamor's proposal and circumcise every male in the city, according to Genesis 34:24.

On the third day after the circumcision, two sons of Jacob's, Simon and Levi, take their swords and go into the city in order to kill every living male. Indeed, they kill all the men of the city, including Shechem and his father, Hamor. They then take Dinah from the house of Shechem and return home with all the wealth of the city and all the females and newborn children they take as captives (Genesis 34:25–29). Now Jacob is afraid that this killing of all the males of the city of Shechem will cause all the neighboring cities around Shechem to attack him. He says to Simon and Levi, in Genesis 34:30, "You have discomposed me, making me all odious among the inhabitants of the land, and I am few in number and could not defend myself if they attacked me and my house."

In other words, Jacob fears that Simon and Levi's actions could bring an end to his household. He does not view the killing of all the males of the city as a good thing. Indeed, he recognizes that although a crime was committed, the punishment has exceeded the specific crime of one man. Many of the men who were killed were innocent in the sense that they did not participate in their prince's action.

However, Simon and Levi are insistent that what was done to their sister has made her like a whore, thereby implying that the punishment fit the crime (Genesis 34:31).

However, Jacob never forgives them and does not speak to them again for what they did to the people of Shechem. Even on his deathbed, he blesses them but still with anger in his blessing.

After these events, God tells Jacob to leave Succoth and come into Beth El, the same place where he saw the angels of God in his dream (Genesis 35:1). Indeed, Jacob orders all the women who Simon and Levi have captured and brought to him, along with their infant children, to remove all the sacrilegious idols from among them, change their clothes, and give him all the rings in their ears in order to cleanse themselves before he takes them to a holy place, meaning Beth El (Genesis 35:2). He then buries all of these things under the terebinth near Shrechem, (Genesis 35:4). Jacob's action implies that earrings and other decorative gold or metal pieces are not welcomed in the presence of God. Note that Genesis 35:4 specifically says that the women of Shechem gave Jacob their idols that were foreign gods and also the earrings and any decorative metals that were on them.

So great was the fear of the people in neighboring cities regarding the killing in Shechem by only two of Jacob's sons, that they dared not attack Jacob's party as they continued toward Beth El (Genesis 35:5).

Once they reach Beth El, Jacob builds an altar to God, and again calls the place the house of God, as he promised to do on his way to Haran (Genesis 35:6–7).

It appears that the fulfillment of Jacob's vow is now complete.

Chapter 18   Jacob Arrives at Beth El

Genesis 35:7 tells us that Jacob arrives at Beth El and builds an altar, and calls the place Beth El. Genesis 35:8 mentions the death and burial of Deborah, the wet nurse or nanny of Rebecca.

The question is what Deborah, Rebecca's nanny, was doing with Jacob.

Note that Beth El is about forty kilometers from Hebron, where Isaac now lives. It appears that when Rebecca found out that Jacob had returned, she sent her nanny to him. Rebecca's nanny must have been very old and just barely able to make the trip from Hebron to Beth El. If Rebecca sent Deborah to Jacob, she herself must not have been able to travel, possibly because she was sick or physically unable to do so. However, when she sends Deborah, it is like making the trip herself. This is very reasonable since Deborah, being Rebecca's nanny, is like her own mother. Also, she must have raised both Jacob and Esau. Because Esau spent most of his time in the fields, she must have been very close to Jacob, as if she were his mother. She also must have wanted to see him before her death, since he was gone for more than twenty years.

In any event, she makes the trip to Beth El and dies there, and Jacob buries her there.

Genesis 35:9–13 tells us that God shows himself to Jacob at Beth El. This is the first time that God shows himself to Jacob while he is awake; at other times that he was with Jacob, he spoke to him only through angels.

In Genesis 35:11, God identifies himself to Jacob as he did to Abraham and Isaac, as El-Shaddai. He then tells Jacob that although he is known as Jacob, he will no longer be called Jacob, but rather Israel. He promises to give the land of Canaan to Jacob and his seeds, and then departs.

Again, Jacob builds a monument, pours oil over it, and names the place the house of God.

Here we see that Jacob's name of Israel is confirmed by El-Shaddai himself, rather than the angel who struggled with Jacob. This confirmation is to eliminate any doubt that Jacob may have about his new name and status, since it came from an angel who sought to stop him from entering the land of Canaan.

Let us examine this event in more detail.

It appears that even if the angel, who has been banished from Eden and tried to stop Jacob from entering into Canaan, decides to change Jacob's name from Jacob to Israel because he fought with Jacob and could not defeat him, his decision is still accepted by the divine. This is an important point: it implies that divine entities must follow certain rules. Even Jacob himself says after wrestling with that angel that he saw God face-to-face and his soul has survived (Genesis 32:31).

This location of Beth El is where Solomon builds the temple for God at today's Jerusalem.

Chapter 19   Jacob settles in Hebron

Jacob and his entire party continue toward Hebron, but Rachel, pregnant with Benjamin, goes into labor on the outskirts of today's Bethlehem (Genesis 35:16). She dies in the process of giving birth. She is able to give the child a name that means "son of my mourning," as if she knows she is dying. However, Jacob names him Benjamin, meaning "son of my right arm" (Genesis 35:18).

Genesis 35:19 tells us that Jacob buries Rachel on the way to Bethlehem, and her grave is a monument for Israel to this day. Note that the tomb of Rachel was to be included in the land of the tribe of Benjamin when Moses divides the land of Canaan among the twelve tribes of Israel.

Jacob continues from Bethlehem toward Hebron and decides to settle at a place called Migdal-Eder, which means "herding tower" (Genesis 35:21). It must have been a place on the outskirts of Hebron where there was sufficient land for all his herds and party.

The Bible tells us that when they settled in that land, Reuben sleeps with Bilhah, Rachel's maidservant, and one of Jacob's concubines (Genesis 35:22). Then the Bible tells us that Israel, meaning Jacob, has heard of this.

Many commentaries over the last several thousand years have tried to mitigate this horrible crime that Reuben committed against his father, Jacob. Most of them claim that Reuben did not actually sleep with Bilhah, but rather slept in his father's bed to demonstrate his annoyance that Jacob chose to stay at Bilhah's tent and not with his mother, Leah.

However, the Bible is clear about this, and there are no ambiguities. Reuben slept with Bilhah, and for this he loses the right of the firstborn that Jacob would have bestowed on him (Genesis 49:4) in Jacob's final blessing to his twelve children. Also note that the tribe of Reuben was pushed beyond the Jordan River into what is the kingdom of Jordan today, as if to say that Reuben was not welcome in the community of Israel.

Now, Isaac lived for many years after Jacob, and his sons arrived at that region around Hebron. It is clear that he knew Joseph and Benjamin and all the sons of Jacob.

The Bible tells us that Isaac died when he was 180 years old (Genesis 35:28), and that Jacob and his brother, Esau, buried him in the cave of Machpelah in Hebron (Genesis 35:29).

At this point, the Bible lists all the descendants of Esau. Note that Esau and his descendants settled in Edom of the ancient world, and south of the kingdom of Jordan of today. As explained earlier, Esau has moved his entire household to Edom because of Jacob's will (Genesis 36:6).

Chapter 20   The story of Joseph

The Bible tells us that Jacob settled in the land of his fathers, the land of Canaan (Genesis 37:1), and continues with a description of Joseph's life. It says that Joseph is seventeen years of age at that point, and that he prefers to spend his time with the sons of Bilhah and the sons of Zilpah (Genesis 37:2). This is very likely since these boys were about his age in comparison to the children of Leah, who were much older. It is also clear that when the Bible mentions Joseph's age, it is with the intention of notifying us that Joseph was a teenager, and that as with any teenager, many of his actions were not measured as if he was an adult.

However, it appears that Joseph and the children of Leah did not get along very well. It is possible that Leah's children felt discriminated against and inferior in comparison to Rachel's children because of Jacob's obvious love for Rachel. They felt that Leah was Jacob's first wife and that they were his elder sons and that they therefore should be treated better and given much more respect and attention than any of the children of Jacob's other wives, including Rachel. However, Jacob clearly favors Joseph over anyone else, and to make matters even worse, he makes Joseph a special fine tunic of different striped colors (Genesis 37:3). The Bible does not mention that he did any such thing for any of his other children.

Obviously, Jacob's special attention to Joseph has caused jealousy and much tension among the children of Leah. As if this was not enough, this special attention from Jacob has caused Joseph to be somewhat spoiled, and he has no problem reporting to Jacob any bad thing that Leah's children have done, according to Genesis 37:2. Clearly, Joseph's actions further infuriate them; the Bible tells us that they literally hated him (Genesis 37:4), and were not able to be friendly with him even to say "Shalom," which is a Hebrew greeting meaning "Peace be on you" and used as commonly as today's hello.

Now, Joseph has a dream, it says in Genesis 37:5, and in his dream he sees all the children of Jacob in a field making sheaves of wheat. Suddenly, Joseph's sheaf of wheat stands erect while the other eleven sheaves bow to it. He then proceeds to tell his brothers about his dream (Genesis 37:7).

The implication is clear: he is telling his brothers that he rules over them, at least in his dream. This does not go well with his brothers, and serves only to intensify their hatred of him (Genesis 37:8). The Bible tells us that Joseph had many other dreams, and he tells his brothers about them, for which they hate him even more. Finally, he has a dream in which he sees the sun and moon and eleven stars bowing before him (Genesis 37:9).

When Jacob hears about this dream, he scolds him and says, in Genesis 37:10, "What is this dream that you have dreamt? Does it mean that I and your mother and your brothers will bow down to you?"

The Bible says that his brothers are jealous of him, and that Jacob keeps the matter to himself.

Let us examine Joseph's dreams in more detail.

It is clear that Joseph is able to connect with the dimension of prophecy, as explained earlier. However, he himself does not understand this connection and his ability to peek into eternity. It is only much later in life that Joseph is able to understand this gift he's been given and use it wisely.

We know that God has shown himself to Jacob at Beth El; thereby he was exposed to the same enlightenment that both Abraham and Isaac were exposed to. That means Jacob must have recognized the special gift Joseph was given. This is why he keeps it to himself, meaning that he is thinking about it and notices that Joseph's dreams are not accidental.

Furthermore, he did not much like Leah's children, because Reuben has committed a grave sin against him by sleeping with Bilhah, and both Simon and Levi have killed innocent men of the city of Shechem. Jacob is looking for the spark of God's light in his children, and he finds it in Joseph.

Now, it came to be that Jacob's elder children took the herds to the lands around Shechem for grazing (Genesis 37:12). This means that Joseph and Benjamin are left behind, because they are the youngest. It is also possible that Jacob keeps Joseph close to him and away from his elder brothers because he is aware of their feelings. Jacob must be aware of the constant complaints that Joseph brings against his brothers.

The reason Jacob's children take the herds north to the lands around Shechem is that it was springtime, and the best grazing grounds for both sheep and goats were around the city of Shechem. The distance between Hebron and Shechem was about seventy to eighty kilometers, which may be considered a long distance; however, if they were going to feed their herds good grass, the land around Shechem was indeed good for that purpose.

Now, the reason that Jacob knows they took the herds to graze around Shechem is again because he knows that these lands are perfect for that.

However, on that special occasion, Jacob asks Joseph to go find out what is going on with his brothers in the fields around Shechem (Genesis 37:14). It must be that Jacob cannot imagine and is not totally aware of the level of hatred that Leah's sons feel for Joseph; otherwise he would not send him to the fields.

The question is, why would Jacob send Joseph, a boy of seventeen, to the city of Shechem, which lies seventy to eighty kilometers from Hebron? After all, this is a substantial distance for a young man to travel alone, and the land was not safe for solitary travel. Jacob could just as easily send one of his servants to see what's going on with his other children.

The answer is that Jacob does not trust any of his servants to tell him the truth about his other children. He knows that they would be influenced by the will of his children and will not tell him the complete truth. Also, since only a few years earlier, two of his sons nearly annihilated an entire city, he does not trust them not to cause more havoc around Shechem.

In Genesis 37:13, he asks Joseph if he would mind being sent to look for his brothers.

Joseph says that he would not mind that at all; indeed, he volunteers for the job. Jacob must know that this area is not safe, but since Joseph has been with his brothers on many such trips, Jacob assumes he is very familiar with the terrain. And because of Joseph's maturity, Jacob assumes he can manage very well by himself even over a distance of seventy to eighty kilometers.

In any event, when Joseph finally reaches Shechem, he is told that his brothers continued to Dothan, which is north of Shechem as shown on the map below (Genesis 37:17).

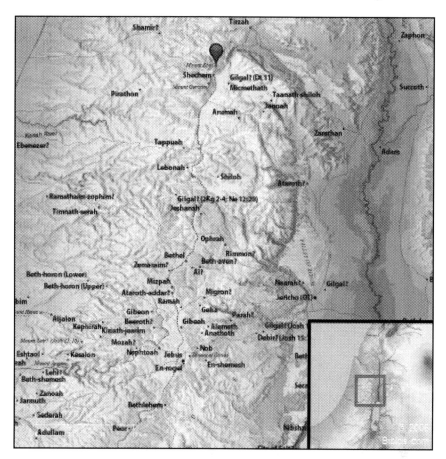

When Joseph finally locates his brothers, they see him from a distance and plot to kill him and then claim that a wild beast has devoured him, saying, "Let us see what comes of his dreams" (Genesis 37:20).

When Reuben hears of the plot, he saves Joseph from them by saying, "We should not kill him but rather throw him into a pit that is in the desert and in this way his blood will not be on our hands." The Bible tells us that Reuben intends to save Joseph later in order to return him to his father (Genesis 37:21–22).

Indeed, the other sons of Leah agree to do as Reuben has suggested. When Joseph approaches them, they grab him, strip him of his coat of many colors, and throw him into a dry well. Then they sit down to eat as if it did not bother them at all (Genesis 37:23–25). It must be noted that during this time Reuben has either finished his lunch and gone back to his herd, or taken the food that they brought to where his herd is. In either case, Reuben is not present and not a witness to or participant in what happens next.

As they finish their lunch, they see a caravan of Ishmaelites approaching their positions that is carrying various spices to sell in Egypt (Genesis 37:25).

The remaining five children of Leah and possibly the four children of Bilhah and Zilpah are all present when this is taking place. However, even though the children of Bilhah and Zilpah are there, they are much younger and cannot resist the will of Leah's children to sell Joseph to the Ishmaelites on the suggestion of Judah.

Judah argues that there would be no benefit in killing Joseph, but by selling him to the Ishmaelites they will make some money. After all, he argued, Joseph is their brother and their own flesh, and in this way their hands will not be stained with his blood. His brothers accept Judah's argument and sell Joseph to the Ishmaelites for twenty pieces of silver, according to Genesis 37:26–28.

When Reuben returns to the dry well where Joseph was held, he finds it empty. Upon seeing the well empty, he rips his clothes and says to his brothers, "The boy is gone, and where would I come?" He means that after the incident between Reuben and Jacob's concubine Bilhah (which Reuben recognizes later to be a grave sin) and now the disappearance of Joseph, his father's beloved son, he, Reuben, has no place to hide. Because he is the eldest son, he is expected to be the leader of Jacob's sons when they are not in the camp (Genesis 37:29–30).

The solution to this dilemma is to kill a goat and dip Joseph's tunic in it in order to mislead Jacob into believing that Joseph was devoured by a wild beast (Genesis 37:31).

Here we see that the sin that Jacob did to his father, Isaac, by lying to him in receiving the blessing of the firstborn has now happened to him by his own sons.

As he deceived his father, he is deceived by his own sons. Note that in both cases, clothing is involved. In the first case, where Jacob deceived Isaac, he used Esau's clothes, whereas in the second case, involving Jacob's sons, they use Joseph's tunic.

Indeed, a crime is punishable exactly as one measure against the other. This punishment for Jacob's action against his father is the basis for one of Moses's laws of an eye for an eye.

Now, Jacob's children bring Joseph's stained tunic to their father and ask him to identify whether it was Joseph's tunic or not. After examining it and recognizing it as Joseph's tunic, Jacob rips his clothes and wears a sack around his waist. He mourns Joseph for many days, saying that Joseph was devoured by wild beasts (Genesis 37:32–34).

Meanwhile, Joseph is sold in Egypt to Potiphar, the courtier of Pharaoh, who was the minister in charge of Pharaoh's kitchen (Genesis 37:36).

At this point, the Bible diverts from the story of Joseph and relates to us the story of Judah.

The reason for this diversion is so the story of the sons of Judah can be told, so that later, when Jacob tells his sons what's going to happen to their seeds at the end of time, one will understand the context.

Chapter 21   The story of Judah

The Bible tells us that sometime later Judah goes to visit his friend from the village of Adullam as shown in the map below (Genesis 38:1). While staying at his friend's house, he meets a woman with whom he falls in love, and indeed he marries her. The woman is the daughter of a Canaanite man known as Shua (Genesis 38:2). Judah's wife gives him three boys, Er, Onan, and Shelah (Genesis 38:3–5).

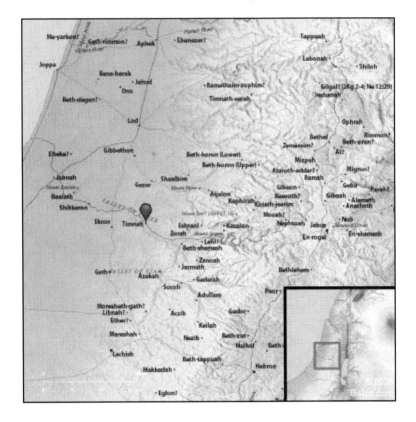

When his eldest son, Er, becomes a man, Judah takes him a wife by the name of Tamar (Genesis 38:6). Now, his son Er is found to be bad in the eyes of the Lord, and the Lord takes his life (Genesis 38:7).

At this point, Judah asks his second son, Onan, to sleep with Tamar so that his brother Er will have descendants on this earth (Genesis 38:8).

Here we see that when a woman marries a man in the ancient world, she also marries his family. It appears that the family members, brothers in particular, are expected to take on the responsibility of giving her their seeds in order to continue their brother's line. This can happen only if one of them dies before she has any children.

Onan obeys his father, but he knows that his seeds will not be his if he makes Tamar pregnant. Therefore, he ensures that his seed does not enter Tamar, and Tamar remains barren. This act of Onan is found to be bad in the eyes of the Lord, and he kills him for it, according to Genesis 38:9–10.

The name Onan in Hebrew has become synonymous with masturbation. We therefore learn that masturbation is forbidden for a man who has a woman, because his seed is considered wasted while denying his wife a child.

Now that Judah has lost two of his three sons, he tells his daughter-in-law to return to her father's house and stay there as a widow until his youngest son, Shelah, grows up (Genesis 38:11). He knows that she can get pregnant only through the seeds of his children as the law of the land demands, but he is afraid that his third son will also die if he gives him to Tamar.

This is where we learn that a woman who buries two husbands is not allowed to wed again.

The Bible tells us that as the years passed, Judah's wife dies (Genesis 38:12). In order to deal with his sadness, Judah joins his men and their herds in the fields of Timnah for the occasion of shearing of the sheep. The shearing of the sheep is a festive occasion accompanied by a feast for the poor.

Timnah was about ten miles northwest of Aczib, where Judah has lived for some time.

It appears that Tamar is told that her father-in-law has gone to shear his sheep in Timnah. She notices that Shelah has become a man and still Judah has not given his son to her. She decides to deceive Judah, and she removes the clothes she was wearing as a widow, replaces them with new clothes, and covers her face with a scarf, as was the custom of prostitutes to hide their identities (Genesis 38:13–14). Her intention is clear; she expects the family of Judah to provide her with seed as she was promised, even if she has to deceive Judah in order to get it.

She then sits on the way leading to Timnah, pretending to be a prostitute (Genesis 38:14). It appears that she arouses Judah's sexual curiosity to the point where he asks her if she will spend the night with him, thinking her to be a prostitute (Genesis 38:16).

When she asks him what he will give her in return, he answers that he will send her a pair of goats from his herd. However, Tamar insists that he give her some sort of a pledge until he sends her the goats. When he asks what that pledge would be, she suggests that he give her his signet, his staff, and the coat of arms he has with him (Genesis 38:17–18).

Judah agrees to her proposal and gives her what she asks for. That night, Judah sleeps with Tamar and she becomes pregnant. In the morning, she leaves the town and returns to her father's house, and again wears her widow's clothing (Genesis 38:18–19).

When Judah sends the pair of goats to this woman by way of his friend, she cannot be found anywhere. His friend keeps asking the people of the town about the prostitute who was sitting on the way to the town, but no one seems to know about such a prostitute. He then returns to Judah and tells him that he cannot find this woman and that no one in the town knows about her either (Genesis 38:20–22).

Judah is worried that his reputation will be tarnished as a man who received services and did not pay for them. He is also worried about the items he gave her, for they are very valuable to him, and pledging them for one night's company with a prostitute will cause people to make fun of him. However, the woman cannot be found.

After several months, Judah is told that Tamar is pregnant, and most likely through prostitution (Genesis 38:24).

In that same verse, he orders that she be brought out and burned. By this command of Judah, we learn that Tamar knew the punishment for having babies out of wedlock. As she is dragged to be burned, she says to her father-in-law, in Genesis 38:25, "By the man to whom these belong I am pregnant. Identify if you please, whose are this seal, this wrap, and this staff."

When Judah sees the three items that belonged to him, he says, in verse 26, "She is right more than me since I did not give her my son Shelah." He then sets her free, and from that day on he is no longer with her.

When the time for delivery arrives, Tamar gives birth to twins. When the first one's hand appears, the midwife wraps a crimson thread around it. However, the second child is delivered first. They call him Perez, and the second one with the crimson thread wrapped around his hand is called Zerah, according to Genesis 38:27–30.

Here again, we learn that God has compensated Judah with two new sons, having taken the lives of two of his sons earlier. Again, a balance has been struck. Also, the ground is being prepared for Jacob's prophecy regarding Shiloh, referred to in Genesis 49:10, which is thought to be the Messiah, who will come out of Judah's original third son, Shelah.

Jacob's prophecies are discussed at length in chapter 22.7.

Chapter 22   Joseph in Egypt

After the story of Judah, the Bible continues the story of Joseph. The reason for the insertion of Judah's story is to teach us the various conclusions drawn in the previous chapter.

As mentioned earlier, in Genesis 37:36, Joseph was sold to Potiphar, the Egyptian minister of food to Pharaoh. The Bible emphasizes that God was with Joseph, and because of that he became successful in his master's house (Genesis 39:2).

When Potiphar sees that Joseph is successful with all things, he realizes that God is with him, meaning that he understands that such success cannot be achieved by the wit of a man without the help of divine intervention (Genesis 39:3).

He then increases Joseph's responsibility and puts him in charge of his entire household and all that he owns. Indeed, God favors the Egyptian with great wealth because of Joseph's presence, as he did with Laban while Jacob was with him, according to Genesis 39:5.

So great is Potiphar's confidence in Joseph that he knows nothing about running his own household or about his wealth, except for the bread that he is given to eat (Genesis 39:6).

What the Bible means by that is that all the accounting, management, and financial matters of Potiphar's estate are taken care of by Joseph, and that Potiphar does not have to be bothered with these things.

The Bible now concentrates on Joseph the young man and says that Joseph was not only good-looking but had a beautiful body (Genesis

39:6). In short, he is very attractive to women. Obviously, having a handsome man in the house of Potiphar does not escape his wife's notice.

She is very attracted to Joseph, and indeed demands that he sleep with her, according to Genesis 39:7. Joseph replies that his master has placed his entire fortune and trust with him and has spared nothing from Joseph except his own wife. How then could he do his master such an evil deed? He will be doing a great sin against his master and against God, which is why he must refuse her (Genesis 39:8–9).

Although she continues to try to seduce him daily, he still refuses (Genesis 39:10).

One day, when Joseph is working inside the house and no other servants are around, she uses this occasion to try to force him into sleeping with her and holds him by his shirt. However, Joseph runs away, leaving his shirt behind with her (Genesis 39:11–12).

She becomes so infuriated and insulted that she raises her voice and calls to the servants of the house. She tells them that "He [meaning Potiphar] brought us a Hebrew man to make fun of us! He came to seduce me and even tried to rape me, but that as soon as I screamed in a loud voice, he ran away and left his shirt behind" (Genesis 39:13–15). She waits until Potiphar comes home from Pharaoh's palace and then tells him the same story (Genesis 39:16–18).

As soon as Potiphar hears his wife's story, he arrests Joseph and puts him in a special jail where the king keeps people who have performed crimes against the king—in short, a white-collar jail (Genesis 39:19–20).

Let us examine this passage in depth.

As we learned earlier, Joseph was given the gift of prophecy, which is evident in his dreams. Therefore, he automatically became a target for the forces of evil. We saw that his brothers tried to kill him and finally threw him into a pit, and again here he is thrown into the king's jail and again into a pit. A pit is typically where snakes can be found. We are speaking here in both physical and spiritual terms.

The question is, who is Potiphar's wife?

As discussed earlier, in chapter 4, the original creation of male and female Adam has the female Adam joining the angel Samael as his companion. She appears many times in human history, mostly in positions of power, either as a queen or in other powerful positions. Here she appears as the wife of Potiphar, trying to seduce Joseph with her extraordinary God-given beauty. After all, she was the first female God created. Very few men, if any, can resist her beauty. However, it appears that Joseph does refuse her advances, and for that he is called a righteous man, or Joseph the Just. In later books of the Bible she appears as Delilah with Samson (Judges 16:4), as Jezebel with King Ahab of Israel (1 Kings 16:31), and as other personalities. Note that her transformation into a flesh-and-blood entity is discussed in chapter 6.

The question is, why did she try to seduce Joseph?

It is clear that if Joseph were truly accused of trying to rape Potiphar's wife, he would be executed immediately. However, because he is only put in prison, it must be that his master, Potiphar, does not want to execute him. After all, such an offense against a minister of the king by one of his servants can easily be punished by death without anyone questioning it. Servants were the property of the master, and if they performed a crime against him, he had the right to execute them.

It is clear that Potiphar does not completely believe his wife, especially knowing Joseph's character and his sense of justice and loyalty. However, because his wife has Joseph's shirt in her possession, he has no choice but to arrest Joseph and put him in jail. It also may be that his wife ripped some of her clothes to further dramatize her situation, thereby forcing his hand to do something about Joseph.

Her hope is to eliminate Joseph and thereby stop any possibility of his descendants becoming Israel's first Messiah. After all, the battle between good and evil has never stopped. Furthermore, any of the promises that God made to Abraham, Isaac, and Jacob would not be able to be fulfilled if Joseph died.

We call Satan's mate Lilith, as discussed earlier in chapter 4. Clearly, that was her intention as was dictated to her by her mate, Satan, or the being that was banished from Eden.

This is the first time we encounter Lilith as Potiphar's wife. However, it is not the last. Oral tradition tells us that Lilith has many names, such as Ishtar, Ashtoreth, Isis, Durga (the wife of Shiva the destroyer), Delilah, Jezebel, and the holy prostitute, as well as Lilith.

She is a female sexual force bent on seducing men to divert them from the path of righteousness. Once they lose their way and their righteousness, they no longer respond to the teaching of God. And once this happens, they are open to all kinds of suggestions from the dark side, including the spilling of blood.

In any event, Joseph is put into the prison supervised by his master, Potiphar. The Bible tells us that God bestows love on Joseph, and his goodness is found to be favorable in the eyes of the prison master (Genesis 39:21).

As we saw earlier, the sefira of love (ח ס ד), or the seventh sefira viewed from the bottom, is considered to be the highest level that any human, even if he was enlightened, can achieve. It appears that the flow of love from a higher level of existence is bestowed on Joseph.

Why is the flow of love from such a high level of existence bestowed on Joseph?

Let us consider this issue. We see that Joseph's status is much lower than that of the prisoners for whom that prison is intended. The prison under Potiphar's supervision is meant to hold high-level dignitaries of the king. Indeed, by placing Joseph into this prison, Potiphar aims to save him from the hard labor that existed in lower-class prisons at that time. Even so, with all of Potiphar's best intentions, Joseph is still a servant and not an Egyptian dignitary. To rise to the status of master supervisor in the prison with the full confidence of the warden of the prison (Genesis 39:22), Joseph must have treated the prisoners with love and care, which the prison warden favored. Because Joseph showed love, mercy, and caring, he caused the flow of those same qualities to be activated from a higher level of existence, namely the seventh sefira of love.

The lesson here is clear: in order to receive love and mercy, one has to give love and mercy to others. In other words, love your neighbor as you love yourself.

Indeed, it seems that Hillel, the Babylonian Jew and Jesus recognized this action many centuries later and both captured its essence in the famous phrase "love your neighbor as you love yourself."

22.1 Joseph's prophecies in the king's jail

Genesis 40:1–3 tells us that after these events, two of Pharaoh's ministers sinned against their king and were sent to the same prison where Joseph was imprisoned and where he also held a supervisory position. Now, Potiphar orders Joseph to serve them personally, since they are ministers of the king and deserve the best treatment while awaiting Pharaoh's judgment. They remain imprisoned for many days (Genesis 40:4).

One night, both these ministers of Pharaoh, the minister of the cupbearers and the minister of the bakers, dream a dream (Genesis 40:5).

When Joseph visits them in the morning, he sees that both of them are very angry. When he asks them, "Why are you angry today?" they reply that they each had a dream but no one can solve them for them (Genesis 40:6–8).

To that Joseph replies, "Only God knows the solutions; however, let me hear your dreams" (Genesis 40:8).

The question is why these ministers would tell Joseph anything at all. After all, he is just a slave and a prisoner of much lower status than themselves.

The answer is that they have seen Joseph getting the respect of everyone in the prison, from the prisoners, to the prison guards, to the warden of the prison himself, and from Potiphar, one of the king's ministers, whom Joseph supposedly wronged. It is clear that if the man you have wronged respects you, it certainly shows that you must be a very special man indeed. They conclude that there is something special about Joseph, and because they see him treating everyone with love and care, they do not hesitate to tell him their dreams.

Furthermore, as noted earlier, Joseph was given the gift of prophecy; he was a seer. Therefore, he is able to peek into the future and see various events unfolding. This ability of Joseph's was evident when he was a teenager; however, as he grew older and matured, he realized that the gift God had given him could be used for good.

We see evidence of the same phenomenon with Abraham, in Genesis 15:12, and with Jacob, in Genesis 28:12. Both of these men were exposed to vivid reality while they were asleep. The connection between deep sleep, which releases the mind from menial tasks in supervising the body and gives it the ability to connect with the dimension of prophecy as explained earlier, and peeking into eternity, is much enhanced. This ability can be manifested in a trance induced by deep hypnosis.

Practitioners of deep trances or states of hypnosis include the yogis of India, Zen priests, the Essene of Israel, American Indian shamans, Christian saints, and others.

However, it is possible that Joseph inherited this special ability through Abraham and Jacob. It is possible that certain areas of some people's brains are much more sensitive to connection with the dimension of universal present than others. The concept of "universal present" is explained earlier in chapter 3.4. The ability to enter into so-called autohypnosis is the necessary first stage, but by itself is not sufficient. One must focus the entire mind and know how to enter the state of prophecy. The process of entering into a state of prophecy is complicated and difficult to master, as was the case with the prophet Samuel as he was training King Saul in this art (1 Samuel 23:6–11).

It appears that Joseph knew about this connection and this ability, and that he further developed it so that he could enter such a state by will. We see evidence of this through the use of a cup that contained water, in Genesis 44:5.

Note that Joseph used water to peek into the dimension of nothingness, as was explained earlier.

The Bible tells us, in Genesis 40:9, that the minister of the cupbearers starts to tell his dream to Joseph first, and that only after seeing that the result of the dream is good does the minister of the bakers volunteer to tell Joseph his dream (Genesis 40:16). This is significant, as we shall see shortly.

The minister of the cupbearers tells Joseph that in his dream he saw a grapevine with three tendrils. He then noticed that the entire grapevine with its tendrils was in full bloom, and that the grapes were ready to be eaten. Then he saw that he was holding Pharaoh's cup in his hands, and that he took the grapes and pressed them into the cup, and handed the cup to Pharaoh (Genesis 40:9–11).

Joseph immediately knows the meaning of this dream. He tells him that in three days Pharaoh will restore him to his previous position and asks him, if he will be so kind to remember him and when God favors him, to speak to Pharaoh in order to get him out of jail. Indeed, Joseph tells him that he was stolen from the land of the Hebrews and brought here, and that even here, he has done nothing to deserve being in this pit (Genesis 40:12–15).

Again, Joseph is able to see the future and therefore act accordingly. He knows that the minister of the cupbearers will be restored to his position; therefore, he asks him to plead his case in front of the Pharaoh. He does not do so with the other minister.

We see evidence of Joseph's ability to see into the future later in Genesis when he tells the people of Israel that upon the date of their freedom from Egypt, they must take his bones with them and bury him in the land of Canaan (Genesis 50:24–25). This ability of Joseph's must have been known within the prison, since it appears that these two ministers of Pharaoh trust whatever he tells them.

After seeing that Joseph has predicted a good outcome for the minister of the cupbearers, the minister of the bakers decides to tell Joseph his dream (Genesis 40:16). However, it must be noted here that the guilty party in any crime does not volunteer information first, but rather waits to see the outcome of the event unfold and whether it is good or bad for him. Had Joseph predicted a bad outcome for the minister of the cupbearers, it is not likely that the minister of the bakers would have spoken at all.

The minister of the bakers tells Joseph that he too had a dream, and in his dream he saw three baskets on his head. They were full of all kinds of delicious bread, and a bird was eating them from the basket (Genesis 40:16–17).

Joseph immediately tells him that within three days Pharaoh will remove his head from his body and then hang his body from a tree to be eaten by birds (Genesis 40:18–19).

Indeed, on the third day of Joseph's prediction, the minister of the cupbearers is restored to his position, and the minister of the bakers loses his head and his body is hanged on a tree for the birds to eat, exactly as Joseph told them, according to Genesis 40:20–22.

The Bible says that the minister of the cupbearers does not remember Joseph and his request after he is restored to his position; indeed, he forgets him altogether (Genesis 40:23).

22.2 Joseph solves Pharaoh's dreams

Genesis 41:1 tells us that two years later, Pharaoh has two dreams. In his first dream, Pharaoh saw himself standing on the bank of the Nile River and observed seven beautiful, healthy cows coming out of the water. They continued to graze on the bank of the Nile. Then he saw another seven cows coming out of the river and approach the seven good-looking cows, which they proceeded to devour (Genesis 41:2–4).

After this dream, Pharaoh woke up. After a while he fell asleep and dreamed another dream. In this second dream, he saw seven ears of healthy, good-looking grain sprouting from a single stalk, followed by seven thin ears of grain that proceeded to eat the seven healthy ones. When Pharaoh wakes up, he realizes it was a dream (Genesis 41:5–7). It appears that the dreams were so real that indeed he thought they were real.

Here we learn that when a divine vision is transmitted to a person in a dream, it appears to him as if it were completely real. We see evidence of this with the prophets of Israel.

However, Pharaoh's spirit is agitated, and he assembles all his wizards and the wise men of Egypt and tells them his dreams so that they can solve them for him. However, no one can provide him with any interpretation, according to Genesis 41:8.

This incident reminds the minister of the cupbearers of the request Joseph made to him, which he has not fulfilled yet. He tells Pharaoh that he must recount his sins today and reminds him of the time when Pharaoh was angry with him and with the minister of the bakers. He then tells Pharaoh that both he and the minister of the bakers had dreams that were solved by a young Hebrew slave who belonged to Potiphar, the minister in charge of food. Then he tells Pharaoh that the dreams were fulfilled exactly as the young Hebrew slave told them (Genesis 41:9–13).

Pharaoh then sends for Joseph from the pit where he is held. Pharaoh's servants change his clothes, shave his head, and bring him in front of Pharaoh (Genesis 41:14).

Now, Pharaoh tells Joseph that he had a dream and that no one can solve it for him, but he understands that Joseph is able to solve dreams (Genesis 41:15).

Joseph replies in the next verse that the solution to Pharaoh's dream is with God only.

Pharaoh relates his dreams to Joseph as described above, and then tells him that none of his wizards can solve them for him (Genesis 41:17–24).

Joseph says to Pharaoh that the two dreams are one and the same, and that God has shown Pharaoh what he intends to do.

He tells him that the seven good cows and the seven good ears of grain represent seven years of plenty, whereas the seven thin cows and the seven thin ears of grain represent seven years of famine.

Joseph advises Pharaoh about what should be done in terms of storing the grain during the seven years of abundance to be used during the years of famine so that Egypt will survive. He tells him to choose a knowledgeable and wise man and put him in charge of this task for all of Egypt, and to provide him with clerical help to collect the grain and store it in all the cities of Egypt. This way, there will be plenty of food in the various cities of Egypt and the people will survive (Genesis 41:25–36).

Pharaoh and his advisers find Joseph's solution to Pharaoh's dream good, and Pharaoh asks his servants and advisers whether they are going to find a man like Joseph who has the spirit of God in him. Then he turns to Joseph and says, "Since God has advised you of these events and there is no one more knowledgeable and wise than you in managing this task, you will be in charge of everything in Egypt, and only by the throne will I be higher than you" (Genesis 41:37–41).

Then Pharaoh removes the ring that was on his hand and gives it to Joseph as a signature and a symbol of the king, and he dresses him with royal robes and places a golden chain around his neck. He gives Joseph his second chariot to ride in and commands that Joseph be referred to as the Blessed One, and he puts him in charge of all Egypt (Genesis 41:42–43).

He tells Joseph that no one in Egypt will be able to do anything without Joseph's permission. In other words, he appoints him as de facto ruler of Egypt.

Pharaoh then changes Joseph's name to Zaphenath-Paneah, which means "solver of mysteries," and gives him the daughter of Poti-Phera, the high priest, for a wife (Genesis 41:44–45).

According to Genesis 41:46, Joseph is thirty years old when he stands in front of Pharaoh.

The question is, how does Joseph know there will be seven years of abundance and seven years of famine?

The answer is that he knew of his father's suffering under his own grandfather Laban when Laban deceived his father, Jacob, for seven years. Jacob considered those the good years, which were followed by seven years of suffering while he waited to have Rachel as his wife. Jacob considered those last seven years the seven bad ones. Note that the cycle of the seven good years followed by seven bad years continues to this day.

Here is one set of data.

On September 11, 1993, Yitzhak Rabin, the prime minister of Israel, and Yasser Arafat, the chairman of the Palestine Liberation Organization, signed a peace agreement in Washington, DC, with Bill Clinton, president of the host country.

For the next seven years, the entire world experienced abundance the likes of which had never been seen in the United States and in many other countries, including Israel. Note that September 11, 1993, was only a few days before the Jewish Rosh Hashanah, which is the Jewish New Year. This date marks the beginning of seven good years.

September 11, 2001, marked the start of seven bad years with the attack on the World Trade Center in New York City. The attack caused a worldwide financial crash and marked the beginning of seven years of suffering. Note that Rosh Hashanah in 2001 was also in September. The cycle of the bad seven years ended with the market crash that began on September 15, 2008, with the collapse of Lehman Brothers. Rosh Hashanah in that year was on September 30, 2008, and began at sundown on September 29, 2008.

There are many such events throughout history, but that is a subject for another time.

The stock market closed on Friday, September 26, 2008, down by 666, at exactly 4:00 p.m. eastern time. One minute later, after all the stock settled, it closed down by 667 points.

It is interesting to note that we associate the number 666 with Satan, and indeed, he is the first angel opposite to Michael, who has a numerical value of twenty-one. Note that the reverse of the names of the seventy-two angels in chapter 10.2 causes the first name to be that of Satan with an equivalent weight of 666. There is no need to repeat his name here in Hebrew. This issue is discussed at length in my book about Exodus, which is currently being written.

To those who understand, the reign of evil ended just before the Jewish Rosh Hashanah, which is the Jewish New Year, and before his term ends, Satan ensures the complete collapse of the financial system of the world. One must note that, for when there is great abundance in the world in the first seven years, it will be followed by great famine and suffering during the next seven years. This means that, as of 2010, we are climbing from the catastrophic depth of famine and suffering into a leveled state—not necessarily into a great position, but certainly a recovery. This recovery will be followed by negative downturn, but not a severe one, during the next seven years.

Let us now return to our subject story.

Joseph knows that Pharaoh's two dreams are indeed one and the same because they were repeated twice to his own father, Jacob (Genesis 29:19 and 27).

Joseph now travels throughout Egypt to set up a program for grain storage. He constructs granaries in each of the cities so that the people of specific areas will be able to get food from them. He then collects so much grain that he stops counting the amount that was collected. The Bible tells us that he collected as much grain as the sand of the sea (Genesis 41:46–49).

22.3 Joseph as viceroy of Egypt

Genesis 41:50–52 tells us that Joseph had two children. The first one was called Manasseth, which means "to forget," for he said that God made him forget the hardship that he suffered in his father's household, and his second son he called Ephraim, which means "fruitful," for he became fruitful in the land of his suffering.

When the seven years of abundance ended, there came seven years of famine as Joseph had predicted, and there was famine throughout the Middle East and the ancient world. But in Egypt there was bread (Genesis 41:53–54).

However, as the famine persisted, the people of Egypt demanded food from Pharaoh, and he told them to go to Joseph and do whatever he told them they must do (Genesis 41:55).

The Bible tells us again that the famine was all over the ancient world and that Joseph opened the granaries and fed the people of Egypt. The fact that Egypt had grain and the rest of the countries did not caused these countries to ask for grain from Egypt. They sent caravans and ships to Egypt in order to buy grain. When Jacob, sitting in Canaan, learns that there is grain in Egypt (Genesis 42:1), he tells his sons not to be afraid, for he has heard that there is grain in Egypt, and that they should travel there to buy some so that everyone will live and not die.

Now it came to be that the ten sons of Jacob, excluding Benjamin, travel to Egypt to buy grain, according to Genesis 42:3. Note here that Judah is among them. This means that the famine is so great that Judah has returned from Aczib to the city of Hebron to be with the rest of his family.

The Bible specifically says that Jacob does not send Benjamin with the rest of his children because he is afraid that an accident might happen to him (Genesis 42:4). Note that Benjamin is nearly thirty-one years old and certainly not a youngster. The reason for this is clear: Jacob does not want to lose the last remaining child of Rachel.

As the children of Jacob, or Israel, wait in line for their turn to buy grain, Joseph, who is in charge of its distribution, recognizes them as they bow before him, although they do not recognize him (Genesis 42:5–7).

The Bible tells us that he speaks to them harshly and demands to know where they have come from. They say that they have come from the land of Canaan in order to buy grain, for there is a great famine in the land (Genesis 42:7–8).

Joseph then remembers all the dreams he used to tell them about, obviously recognizing that those dreams have come true. However, he accuses them of being spies who have come to survey the land and possibly learn about Egypt's weaknesses (Genesis 42:9). Note that Egypt was at constant war with the Hittites, who were of the region extending from today's Turkey to Israel, and that these ten people came from that land, so Joseph uses that as an excuse for his accusations.

They said to him, "No my Lord, we came to buy grain. We are all from the same father. We are not liars, and we are your servants, not spies" (Genesis 42:10).

However, Joseph insists that they are spies who came to survey the land (Genesis 42:12).

Then they answered him and said, "We are twelve children of the same father, and the youngest one stayed behind in the land of Canaan with our father, and another one is missing" (Genesis 42:13).

But Joseph says to them, "As I said before, you are spies, and this will be your test in the name of Pharaoh: you will not leave this place unless you bring me your youngest brother. Let one of you return and bring your youngest brother while you are held in prison to be interrogated in order to find out if you are speaking the truth about being spies."

He then places them under guard for three days (Genesis 42:14–17).

On the third day, Joseph decides to speak to his brothers. He tells them that he is a God-fearing man and that it is possible that they are speaking the truth. If so, one of them can remain behind while the rest can go back and take grain to their families. However, if they bring back their youngest brother, they can be trusted and will not be put to death (Genesis 42:18–20).

Indeed, his brothers accept the proposal, according to Genesis 42:20.

It is clear that Joseph uses many interpreters for various people coming from different countries and speaking different tongues. It is also clear that in this case, he uses an interpreter who speaks both Hebrew and Egyptian. Since they accept his proposal, there is no longer any need for an interpreter. Although Joseph may still be within hearing range, they assume he does not understand their language, and they feel free to speak among themselves in Hebrew and Aramaic.

Genesis 42:21–23 tells us that they blame themselves for not listening to Joseph's pleas to let him go after they threw him into the pit years before, and because of this sin of theirs, this disaster has happened to them now. They do not know that Joseph understands their language, because he spoke to them through an interpreter.

As Joseph hears them speaking among themselves, he turns away behind a wall and cries, unable to hold back his emotions any longer. Once he regains his composure, he returns to speak to them and arrests Simon in front of their eyes (Genesis 42:24).

Here we learn again that any act of evil will be balanced by another act, a measure against a measure. The balance is restored.

Note that as his brothers captured Joseph and threw him into a pit, one of them now is arrested and thrown into a pit. It appears that Joseph's choice of Simon is not accidental; it most likely is Simon who wanted Joseph killed in the first place.

After the arrest of Simon, Joseph orders his staff to fill their sacks with grain and to put the money that each one of them brought to buy grain back in their sacks. He does this without his brothers knowing about these actions. He further orders that they be given sufficient food for the journey back to Canaan (Genesis 42:25).

Joseph's brothers travel back until nightfall, and then they stop and prepare to sleep for the night at one of the inns on the way. As one of them opens his sack to feed the animals, he notices that all the money he gave to the Egyptians is back in his sack.

He immediately tells his brothers about this and they all are very concerned, because they do not understand what is happening. However, they continue toward Canaan to bring food to their families (Genesis 42:26–29).

When they reach the land of Canaan and the house of Jacob, they tell their father all that has happened to them, including the fact that the ruler of Egypt suspected them of being spies. They tell Jacob that he retained Simon in a prison in Egypt and sent them back to bring food to their families. The Egyptian ruler told them to bring their younger brother back with them if they were speaking the truth about them not being spies, and said that he will not see them unless they bring back their younger brother with them.

However, on the way back, they found money in one of their sacks.

When Jacob himself examines their sacks and finds the money there, they all become fearful (Genesis 42:30–35).

Then Jacob says to them (Genesis 42:36) "Is it not enough that I have lost Joseph, and now Simon, and you want to take Benjamin too?"

Now then, Reuben says to his father, in the next verse, "You can kill my two sons if you give me Benjamin and I do not return him to you" (Genesis 42:37). However, Jacob does not accept Reuben's proposal. The reason is clear: he does not trust Reuben at all. After what he did with Bilhah, and after losing Joseph while he was the elder one responsible for the entire group, it's no wonder that Jacob considered Reuben's word worthless.

This state of affairs remains until they finish all the grain in their possession. Once the grain is gone, Jacob has no choice but to reconsider sending them back to Egypt.

Genesis 43:2 tells us that when Jacob asks them to go back to Egypt to buy more grain, Judah takes the initiative and tells his father that they dare not show their faces to the master of the land without their younger brother. After all, they were told plainly that they could not see his face again without their younger brother. However, if Jacob will send their youngest brother with them, they can bring back food (Genesis 43:4).

Jacob then asks them why they told this master of the land that they have another brother. They answer that the man asked them while they were held under guard if they had a living father and other brothers, as if he knew they had other brothers and a living father. They told him the truth; for how did they know he would ask them to bring their brother back with them? (Genesis 43:6–7).

Note here that the Bible uses the name Israel instead of Jacob (Genesis 43:6, 8, and 11).

Judah then says to Jacob (Genesis 43:8–9) "Send the boy with me and I guarantee to you that I will bring him back without any harm to stand before you, and if I do not, then I have committed a sin against you for the rest of my life."

It appears that Jacob accepts Judah's proposal, and the brothers prepare to leave the camp (Genesis 43:11).

The question is, why does Jacob accept Judah's proposal and not Reuben's?

As explained earlier, he didn't think Reuben's proposal had merit, but when it came to Judah, he accepted his proposal. This is because of the fact that Judah had never sinned against anyone, and when he was mistaken, he admitted his mistakes and did not hide them. By doing this, he gained his father's respect and trust.

Now, Jacob tells his children that if this is to be, they must take a tribute to this man that will include wax lotus, pistachios, almonds, and honey. He also tells them to take twice the money they took before, including the money that was returned to them; possibly because the Egyptians made a mistake, and therefore, it must be returned (Genesis 43:11–12).

As Jacob sends his children on their way, he blesses them and asks El-Shaddai to give them mercy and to return Benjamin and their other brother with them (Genesis 43:14).

Note that Jacob does not mention Simon by name, even though it is clear that he knows Simon is being held in Egypt. This shows that Jacob's anger with Simon is still there, to the point that he doesn't even mention his name.

After this event, the ten children of Jacob travel to Egypt to stand before Joseph together with Benjamin. When Joseph sees Benjamin with them, he tells the master in charge of his household to prepare a feast and bring these people to his house to have lunch with him (Genesis 43:15–16).

Indeed, the master of the house does exactly as Joseph ordered him and brings all ten men to Joseph's house for lunch.

When Joseph's brothers are brought to the house, they think a trap is being set for them and become fearful because of the money that was found in their sacks (Genesis 43:18).

So they engage the master of Joseph's house and speak to him before they enter, saying that they came to Egypt the first time to buy grain, and that when they stopped for the night and opened their sacks to feed the animals, they found the money in their sacks, and that they brought it back with them, as well as additional money to buy new grain (Genesis 43:19–22).

Then the master of Joseph's house tells them to be in peace and not to be afraid. He says their God must be the one who gave them the money they found in their sacks, and that it is theirs to keep. Furthermore, he releases Simon to them as a sign that he holds no grudge or anger toward them.

He then brings them inside the house, brings them water to wash their feet and faces, and takes their donkeys to be fed (Genesis 43:23–24).

As they are waiting to have lunch with Joseph, as they were told by the master of the house, they prepare the tribute that Jacob sent with them (Genesis 43:25).

When Joseph comes to the house and joins them, they give him the tribute that they brought with them and bow down to him. When Joseph sees them bowing before him, all eleven of them, he knows that the dream he had about the eleven sheaves of wheat when he was seventeen has now been fulfilled.

He bids them peace, which was a customary exchange in the Middle East at that time and is to this day, and then asks them if their old father is still alive. They bow down again and reply that his servant, their father, is still alive (Genesis 43:26–28).

When Joseph focuses his attention on Benjamin, he asks them if this is the younger brother they spoke of and then he says to him, "God bless you, my son" (Genesis 43:29).

Seeing all his brothers with him in the same room, and seeing his brother Benjamin, whose features are like those of his mother, Rachel, Joseph quickly leaves the room, unable to hold back his emotions, and goes into another room to cry. After he regains his composure, he washes his face and returns to the room where his brothers are (Genesis 43:30–31).

Then he orders that bread be brought to everyone in the room, including the Egyptian staff (Genesis 43:31–32).

In the Middle East, it is customary to have the bread put in front of everyone. When a person wants a piece of bread, he takes a slice of a larger round, thin bread, similar to pita bread, while leaving the other portion on the same tray. However, the Egyptians did not like to share bread in this way with the Hebrews, possibly because they considered them to be shepherds, as compared with the Egyptians, who were cowherds. It appears that the feud between shepherds and cowherds, which was well known in the Midwest of the United States, is as old as Joseph's time.

This is why Joseph orders his staff to place separate bread for himself, the Hebrews, and the Egyptians.

Now, Joseph has arranged the sitting of his brothers in accordance with their ages. When they realize that they are seated in the order of their birth, they are perplexed, according to Genesis 43:33.

Joseph gives them wine to drink and gives Benjamin five times as much as the others. It is clear that wine, even in those days, was used as a means to celebrate and to toast specific occasions. By giving Benjamin five times as much wine as his other brothers, Joseph makes the point that he values Benjamin more than his other brothers, possibly to see if the jealousy that his brothers harbored for the children of Rachel was still there (Genesis 43:34).

When they finish eating, Joseph orders his staff to fill his brothers' sacks with grain, and for his silver cup to be placed in Benjamin's sack, together with the money that Benjamin brought to buy grain. Clearly, none of the brothers know about this (Genesis 44:1–2).

In the morning, his brothers leave the compound on their way back to Canaan. As soon as they leave the city, Joseph orders his guards and the master of his household to chase the Hebrews and, when they reach them, to say, "Why have you done evil to my master after the good he did to you, that you have taken the silver cup that my master uses to see the future? Indeed you have done evil this day" (Genesis 44:3–5).

Here we see again that Joseph has used the silver cup with water in it to gaze into the future through the sefira of prophecy. Note that Nostradamus, who was born a Levite, in France, used the same method.

When Joseph's brothers hear these accusations, they say it would be sacrilegious for them to do those things, as evidenced by the fact that they have returned the money they found in their sacks the first time they came to buy grain. Why would they steal silver or gold from the master this time? However, they continue, he who has stolen such a cup will die, and they all will be slaves to your master (Genesis 44:7–8).

The master of Joseph's house replies that there is no justification in all of them becoming slaves, but only the one found with the cup will become a slave (Genesis 44:10).

Joseph's brothers quickly unload the sacks off their donkeys and proceed to open them so that the master of Joseph's house can search each one of them.

The master begins his search with Reuben, being the eldest, and finishes with Benjamin, being the youngest.

When he finds the cup in Benjamin's sack, all the brothers rip their clothes, and they reload the sacks of grains on their donkeys and return to the city with the master of Joseph's house (Genesis 44:11–13).

The Bible tells us that it is Judah and his brothers who return to Joseph's house, meaning that now it appears that Benjamin is in trouble; it is Judah who assumes the responsibility for his safety as he promised his father, Jacob (Genesis 44:14).

Indeed, when they return to Joseph's house, Joseph is still there. As they approach him, they all bow before him. Then he says to them, "Why have you done such a thing? Did you not know that a person like me would be able to find the truth?" (Genesis 44:14–15).

What Joseph means here is that he is well known in Egypt as a sort of a prophet or seer of the future, and therefore nothing would be hidden from him. It should have been obvious to them, therefore, that he would know what they have done.

Judah answers him and says, "What can we say to my lord, and how can we justify ourselves? God has uncovered the sin of your servants; we are ready to be slaves to my lord, including him with whom the cup was found" (Genesis 44:16).

Now, Joseph replied to them and says, "It would be sacrilegious for me to do this. Only the man who possessed the cup will be a slave to me; the rest of you can go back to your father in peace" (Genesis 44:17).

Judah, who is responsible for Benjamin, approaches Joseph and says, "If you please, my lord, may your servant speak and let not your anger flare up at your servant, for you are like Pharaoh." He means that he considers Joseph comparable to the king of Egypt, and that if Joseph gets angry, he may order Judah's execution, as we've seen earlier with the two ministers of Pharaoh. In other words, Judah is asking Joseph permission to speak freely without being punished for his boldness.

It appears that Judah continues with a description of what happened to Jacob and his children without waiting for approval from Joseph. It is also possible that Joseph nodded in approval or gestured for Judah to continue. A hand gesture of approval in the Middle East was a common sign to continue.

Judah outlines the recent events since famine has struck the land of Canaan. He tells Joseph that when Joseph asked them if they had a father or brother, they told him that they did have both an old father and a young brother, the only one remaining since his older brother died and whom their father loved very much.

"Now then, you have told us to bring our youngest brother to you so that you can see him and believe that we are not spies. Furthermore, you told us that if we did not bring our youngest brother with us, we could not see you and you would not grant us access to the grain that we need to survive.

"When we told our father all that you said to us, our father said to us that we knew that his wife gave him two sons and that the elder one left his house and was devoured by a wild beast. If we take this one from him and an accident happens to him, he said, we will surely drive him to the grave.

"Now, if we return to our father without the boy, knowing that his soul is tied up with the boy's soul, we will surely bring death upon him. Since I guaranteed the boy's safety, let me be a slave for you instead of the boy, for I cannot see my father die in front of me" (Genesis 44:18–34).

After hearing Judah's plea, Joseph cannot control his emotions any longer. He orders all the Egyptian staff with him to leave the room immediately. Once they leave the room, Joseph bursts out crying. So loud is the sound that the Egyptian staff outside the room hear him cry and notify the house of Pharaoh, since they do not understand why Joseph is crying. However, since Joseph does not ask for help, they don't dare enter the room.

Joseph's outburst scares his brothers, for they do not understand why he is crying either. After all, why would the king of Egypt cry in front of them, and why would he ask his Egyptian staff to leave the room?

When he is finally able to speak, he tells them that he is Joseph, and the first question he asks is, "Is my father still alive?" (Genesis 45:1–3).

Imagine how stunned his brothers are when he tells them that he is Joseph. After all, they have seen him on many occasions now, and none of them was able to recognize him as Joseph. They simply cannot believe their ears or eyes.

When Joseph sees that they are afraid of him, he tells them again that he is Joseph and to come closer to him. He says to them that he is their brother Joseph, whom they sold as a slave to Egypt, and that they shouldn't be sad or angry about it, for God sent him ahead of them so that all will survive (Genesis 45:4–5).

He tells them that the famine is in its second year and it will last for five more years, and that God has sent him to Egypt in order to provide for them so that they can survive. He said that they were not the ones who sent him here; but it was God who appointed him as second-in-command to Pharaoh and ruler of all Egypt.

Joseph then asks his brothers to hurry back to his father and tell him all that they have heard, and that he should come to Egypt and settle in the land of Goshen. That way, he and all his children and grandchildren and all that he owns will be close to Joseph so that he can feed and take care of them. Joseph tells them to notify his father that the famine will last for five more years, and that he is afraid that if Jacob is not close to him, he may perish (Genesis 45:6–11).

While his brothers are still in shock, he hugs his brother Benjamin and they cry together on each other's shoulder. Then he kisses and hugs all his brothers until they relax enough to speak to him (Genesis 45:14–15).

When Pharaoh hears that Joseph's brothers are with him, he tells Joseph to tell his father and brothers and all their families to come to Egypt and settle there, and that he will give them the best Egypt can offer. He gives them wagons so that they can carry their children and wives back from Canaan.

Joseph does as Pharaoh commands him. He gives his brothers wagons to use while traveling and enough food and supplies for the trip in both directions. He then gives them new suits, and to Benjamin he gives three hundred silver pieces and five new suits, and to his father he sends ten donkeys carrying the best Egypt can offer and ten she-donkeys loaded with grain and bread and food for the trip back from Canaan to Egypt.

Then he sends his brothers on their way and tells them not to quarrel during the trip to Canaan. Joseph understands that his brothers may quarrel among themselves and blame each other for selling him into slavery (Genesis 45:16–24).

Let us consider this passage carefully.

We see that even though Joseph is sold into slavery, thrown into jail, and suffers for thirteen years, he does not hold a grudge against his brothers.

The question is, why? After all, it would be completely normal to be angry with the people who tried to kill you and sell you as a slave to a foreign land. Why does Joseph forgive them and not get angry with them?

The answer is that Joseph has seen the future and realized that their actions were dictated by a higher power, and that they were doing only what they were supposed to do. Furthermore, Joseph has attained a level of enlightenment that allows him to be merciful and to shed any negativity or the desire to destroy.

Since he practiced this understanding while he was in prison with strangers, how could he not practice it with his own brothers?

That is why he tells his brothers that it was all ordained by God.

22.4 Joseph is still alive

When his brothers reach Jacob's compound, the first thing they tell their father is that Joseph is still alive and that he is the ruler of all Egypt (Genesis 45:26).

Oral tradition tells us that Serach, daughter of Jacob's son Asher, was sent ahead of the brothers into Jacob's tent to play a harp and to gently mention that Joseph is alive and that he is ruler of Egypt. It appears that Jacob's sons want to notify their father that Joseph is alive in a gentle way so that he will not have a heart attack and die when he hears the news.

It is said that indeed Jacob's spirit was relaxed when he heard the music of the harp and that he blessed his granddaughter Serach for trying to soothe his spirit. Tradition tells us that because of Jacob's blessing, Serach lived for several centuries and that she was the one who pointed out Joseph's grave when the people of Israel were ready to leave Egypt with Moses (Zohar).

In any event, when the sons of Jacob tell him that Joseph is still alive, he is not prepared to believe them. However, after they describe everything that happened and he sees with his own eyes what Joseph has sent back with them, his spirit becomes alive (Genesis 45:27). Once his spirit is revived, he is called Israel again instead of Jacob. It appears that since the time when Joseph was thought to be dead, his father's spirit was too; for twenty-two years, he was called Jacob. However, when Jacob finds out that Joseph is alive, his spirit becomes alive, too, and he is called Israel again. He says that now that my son Joseph is still alive, I will go and see him before I die (Genesis 45:28).

Here we learn that the bond between father and son is not only physical but also spiritual, and if the child dies, the parent feels dead too.

Note that Jacob's name is confirmed to be Israel at the event when "El-Shaddai" shows himself to him at Beth El, in Genesis 35:10–13.

Since that time and until Joseph is sold to Egypt and Jacob believes that he is dead, the Bible refers to him as Jacob (Genesis 37:28; 42:1, 29, 36). Only when his children stand in front of Joseph on their trip to secure grain from Egypt and when Joseph recognizes them to be his brothers does the Bible refer to Jacob as Israel (Genesis 43:6, 8; 45:27–28). Also note that in Genesis 37:1–2, even though the Bible uses the name Jacob, it is used to describe Jacob's chronicles (history) and is not connected to any of his actual actions.

22.5   Israel settles in Egypt

Genesis 46:1 tells us that Jacob assembles all that he has and starts his journey toward Egypt. On his way from Hebron, he stops at Beersheba, where both Abraham and Isaac lived for a long time. He then sacrifices an offering to the God of Isaac, his father. Again, the Bible mentions the God of Isaac only and not the God of Abraham.

This is because Jacob is appealing to the sixth sefira of might, since he needs the mighty hand of God to accompany him and keep him and his family safe on his journey to Egypt. Note that when he sends his children on their second trip back to Egypt, he blesses them with mercy, which was the seventh sefira (Genesis 43:14). This means that he appealed to the love and mercy of God to be with his children on their trip back to Egypt.

These two specific examples of Jacob appealing to a specific attribute of God show us that he was very familiar with the different aspects of the ten sefirot or emanations of God. Indeed, we see that Isaac was familiar with the same thing, since he appealed to the sefira of foundation, which is the second sefira, when Rebecca was barren and could not have children (Genesis 25:21).

God's sixth attribute, the attribute of might, shows itself that same night and tells Jacob not to be afraid of going down to Egypt. He will be with him all the time, and when he dies, Joseph will be the one to close the lids of his eyes. God promises him that he will bring him back from Egypt to be buried in Canaan together with his father (Genesis 46:2–4).

This is extremely significant, since it shows us that Abraham, Isaac, and Jacob understood the complexities of the attributes of God and they appealed to different ones, for different purposes, depending on their need.

Since Joseph was gifted with access to the attribute of prophecy, even though Jacob may not have yet explained the complexities of God's attributes to him, it appears that he was able to figure this out on his own.

It is possible that in the remaining seventeen years of his life, Jacob transmitted his knowledge of the attributes of God to Joseph; however, there is no indication in the Bible that God has made contact with Joseph either verbally or by sight, only that he was with him and blessed him.

Now that Jacob has received God's promise to be with him and his family, he continues to Egypt without any fear, according to Genesis 46:5.

The Bible tells us that the entire family of Jacob, including that of Joseph, totaled seventy people in all (Genesis 46:8–27). The significance of this number is discussed in chapter 10.2. Since the Bible does not mention any of Jacob's wives, it must be that all of them have passed away by this time. This can be easily understood, because Jacob was 130 years old, and any of his wives would be more than one hundred years old; therefore it is possible that all of them have passed away. No mention is made in the Bible of the deaths of Leah, Zilpah, or Bilhah.

It appears that Leah's daughter, Dinah, did not marry or have children after she was raped by Shechem, the son of Hamor, and the Bible mentions her as an individual without naming any children (Genesis 46:15).

Genesis 46:28 tells us that Jacob sends Judah ahead of him to the land of Goshen. Here we see again that Jacob chooses Judah to be the leader of the rest of his brothers and to pick the place for their settlement. It appears that Jacob chooses him and that his brothers accept him as the natural leader of the house of Israel.

When they finally arrive at Goshen, Joseph hurries up to meet his father; when they see each other, they fall on each other's shoulders and cry for a long time. Then Jacob tells Joseph that now that he has seen him, he can die in peace (Genesis 46:29–30). Now, Joseph assembles the entire household of Jacob and tells them that he is going back to Pharaoh to tell him that his brothers and his father's household have come to him from the land of Canaan, and that they brought with them all they have, including sheep and cows. Now, if Pharaoh asks them what they intend to do in Egypt, they should tell him that they have been shepherds for many generations (Genesis 47:31–34).

Joseph knew the Egyptians did not like to be in the presence of shepherds; therefore, they would prefer that the Hebrews settle in Goshen some distance away from them, which is exactly what Joseph wanted. In this way, Joseph tries to keep his father's house from any exposure to the Egyptian culture.

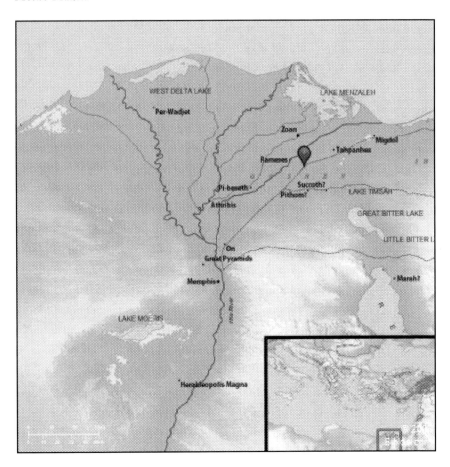

After informing his brothers about what to say in front of Pharaoh, Joseph picks five of his brothers who do not look like warriors with strong body build and presents them to Pharaoh (Genesis 47:2). Joseph knows that if he picks some of his other brothers, such as Judah, who have strong, muscular bodies, they might be drafted into Pharaoh's army.

Indeed, when he presents them to Pharaoh and tells Pharaoh that his brothers and his father's household have come to Egypt and they are in Goshen, Pharaoh asks his five brothers with him about their occupation, and they tell him that they have been herders of sheep for many generations (Genesis 47:3).

When Pharaoh hears this, he tells them to settle in the land of Goshen, as Joseph predicted, so that there will be enough food for their sheep. He tells Joseph that if any among his brothers is fit to serve in his army, he can be in charge of Pharaoh's many herds (Genesis 47:6). Clearly, Pharaoh does not consider the five men standing in front of him capable of managing his many herds.

The question is, did Joseph know exactly what was going to happen when he brought his five brothers to Pharaoh? Or was it just a good plan?

Since we have seen that Joseph could see the future, it is reasonable to assume that he saw all that would happen and instructed his brothers accordingly.

Joseph then proceeds to present his father, Jacob, to Pharaoh, and when Jacob stands before him, Pharaoh asks him his age. Jacob replies that he is 130 years old, that these years were short and bad, and that they did not come close to the lives of his father and grandfather (Genesis 47:7–9).

The Bible tells us that Jacob blesses Pharaoh and then leaves to go back to Goshen, and that Joseph has given Jacob and his household plots of land from the best of the land of Ramses, being the land of Goshen (Genesis 47:10–11).

Note that this is the first time we find out that the name of this Pharaoh is Ramses. Since all of the land of Egypt belonged to him, the Bible says that Jacob and his household were given plots of lands in the land of Ramses.

Why did Joseph pick five of his brothers to present to Pharaoh?

Note that this is actually the third time Joseph uses the number five. The first time is when he gives Benjamin five portions of wine, the second time is when he gives Benjamin five new suits, and the third time is when he picks five of his brothers to be presented to Pharaoh. There is another time just ahead in Genesis where Joseph uses the number five again. That fourth time is when he gives the farmers one-fifth of the crops, as we shall see shortly (Genesis 47:24).

Joseph used the fifth sefira from the bottom, knowing that it is the balance between the seventh attribute of God, which is love, and the sixth attribute of God, which is might and judgment, as viewed from the bottom of the Tree of Life. He knew that using the balance between these two extremes was the only thing they could do to ensure survival.

Indeed, oral tradition teaches us that Joseph was considered to be the foundation, because of the fact that he saved the ancient world. The oral tradition associates names of specific individuals with specific sefira. In this way, the seventh sefira is associated with Abraham, the sixth sefira is associated with Isaac, and the fifth sefira is associated with Jacob.

After these events, the Bible tells us that the famine in Egypt and in the land of Canaan had become extreme. Joseph collects all the money from the people in exchange for the grain that he gave them and gives the money to Pharaoh (Genesis 47:14).

When all the money in the land dries up and the people cannot pay for their grain, they come to Joseph and demand it. However, he tells them they can buy grain in exchange for their herds and donkeys. In this way, they survive that year (Genesis 47:15–17).

When all the herds and all their possessions excluding their lands are used to buy grain, they sell their land to Joseph, who gives it to

Pharaoh in exchange for the grain that they receive (Genesis 47:18–20).

Now that the land of Egypt legally belongs to Pharaoh, Joseph moves all the people from the countryside into the cities. In this way, no one will have a claim on the land, since it is not his any longer. The only exception is the land and the grain that is given to the priests of Egypt, since it is given to them by Pharaoh (Genesis 47:21–22).

When all the land of Egypt is under Pharaoh's control, Joseph gives the people seeds to plant in anticipation of the end of the famine at the end of the seventh year. Joseph knows exactly when the famine will end; therefore he knows it is time to plant the fields.

However, he establishes that one-fifth of the harvest on the land will be the people's share, whereas the other four-fifths of the harvest will be for Pharaoh. This law of Joseph's is still valid to this day (Genesis 47:23–26).

This sentence points out the potential date for the writing of the Bible. It says that the law of Joseph was still valid to this day, meaning until the people of Israel leave Egypt at the time of Moses. This confirms that these five books of the Old Testament were indeed written by Moses around 1250–1500 BC.

The Bible tells us that Jacob, now called Israel, has settled in the land and multiplied greatly (Genesis 47:27).

Note that Jacob is now referred to as Israel (Genesis 47:27–29). However, when his chronicles are described, the name Jacob is used, and when he is referred to in the third person, he is called Jacob (Genesis 48:2).

22.6 Jacob blesses Joseph, Ephraim, and Manasseh

Genesis 47:27–31 tells us that when Jacob is 147 years of age, and knows his time to die is near, he summons his son Joseph and makes him swear that he will not be buried in Egypt, but rather with his father and grandfather in Canaan. Joseph vows to do as he is asked.

Sometime later, Joseph is notified that his father is indeed very sick, and he knows that his father's time to die is approaching. He takes with him his two sons, Manasseh and Ephraim, and comes to his father (Genesis 48:1).

When Jacob is told that his son Joseph is coming to see him, he is strengthened and sits upright on his bed (Genesis 48:2).

When they are together, Jacob relates to Joseph all that has happened to him, including the fact that God—El-Shaddai—appeared to him in Luz, which was later called Beth El, and promised him to give the land of Canaan to him and his seed forever. However, he tells Joseph that his two sons belong to him against Simon and Levi. He tells him that they will inherit their share in the land of Canaan, and any other children that Joseph may have will belong to Joseph (Genesis 48:3–6).

What Jacob means here is that he considers both Simon and Levi lost to him, and he has replaced them with Joseph's sons. Indeed, he has never forgiven these two for what they did in Shechem.

Then he tells Joseph about his mother, Rachel. It appears that he is apologizing for burying her outside Bethlehem and not with the gravesite of his parents. As he speaks, he notices the two boys next to Joseph and asks him who they are (Genesis 48:7–8).

Joseph says they are the sons God has given him. Jacob then asks Joseph to bring them closer to him so that he can bless them, since his eyes are dim and he cannot see well.

Joseph brings them closer to his father, and Jacob hugs and kisses them. Then Jacob tells Joseph that he did not expect to see his face again while he was alive, and certainly not his children.

Then Joseph removes the boys from between Jacob's knees and bows down to him. He takes Ephraim in his right hand and Manasseh in his left hand and presents them to his father (Genesis 48:9-13).

Joseph intends to have Jacob bless his older son with his right hand and his younger son with his left hand. However, Jacob crosses his hands and places his right hand on the head of Joseph's youngest son, Ephraim, and his left hand on the head of Joseph's older son, Manasseh, according to Genesis 48:14.

He then blesses Joseph first and says, "The God of my fathers, Abraham and Isaac, and the God who guided me since I was born, the angel that saved me from all evil, bless these boys and my name will be called in them, and my father's names, Abraham and Isaac, will be declared upon them, and may they multiply upon the earth" (Genesis 48:15–16).

When Joseph sees that Jacob's hands are crossed, and that he is blessing the younger one with his right hand, which is considered a more favorable blessing, he tries to remove Jacob's hand from the head of his youngest son. However, Jacob refuses and says he knows who is whom, and that indeed the older son will be a mighty nation; however, the younger son will be mightier, and his seeds will fill the nations of the earth. Then he blesses them and says that the people of Israel will bless each other, saying, "May God make you like Ephraim and Manasseh" (Genesis 48:17–20).

Then Jacob tells Joseph that he is dying and that God will be with all of them, that he will return them to the land of their fathers, and that he, Jacob, has given Joseph the city of Shechem that he took from the Amorites (Genesis 48:21–22).

22.7   Jacob's prophecies for the end of time

Jacob calls for the rest of his children and tells them to assemble around him before he dies so that he can tell them what will happen to them at the end of days (Genesis 49:1–2).

He speaks to them as follows:

"Reuben,

"You are my firstborn, my strength, and my vigor; you are first in rank and first in might. However, your actions without much deliberation are like water. They are lost if they are not collected, for you have mounted your father's mate and by that you have desecrated my bed" (Genesis 49:3–4).

Here, Jacob tells Reuben in plain words what Reuben has done to him and how he feels about it. Jacob uses the analogy of water since he knows that his sons, being shepherds in the southern desert of Israel, understand perfectly the importance of managing water to survive. Obviously in somewhat dry land, one must learn to preserve water by preparing the means to collect it, store it in specific places, and use it intelligently. What Jacob is telling Reuben is that he should have used deliberation and thinking to be aware of his actions. Otherwise, they are like the abundance of water, which gives life but if not managed properly will seep into the ground and be lost.

To Simon and Levi he said,

"Simon and Levi are brothers, and their tools are those of destruction. Let my spirit not share in their secrets. In their congregation my honor is not respected, for in their rage they killed people, and by their will they maimed an ox. Their rage is cursed, and their wrath is hard. I will divide them in Jacob and disperse them in Israel" (Genesis 49:5–7).

It is clear that Jacob has never forgiven these two sons for what they did in Shechem. The first passage, which speaks of using their weapons as tools of destruction, refers to the killing of all the males in Shechem.

The second statement refers to the conspiracy between them regarding the plan to kill Joseph. This is why Joseph retains Simon in jail while he sends the other brothers back to Canaan.

The third statement refers again to the promise that Jacob made to the people of Shechem about the circumcision of all the males in the city, thereby becoming one people with Jacob. He blames both Simon and Levi for dishonoring him by their actions.

In the fourth statement, Jacob explains the reason for his harsh words. He tells them that they have killed innocent people, even though they knew that only Shechem, the son of Hamor, was guilty for the evil done to their sister, Dinah. Furthermore, he tells them that by their will they maimed an ox, meaning that he witnessed them sterilizing an ox, which was against God's law.

Finally, he prophesies their future. He tells them that their rage is cursed and evil and that he will divide them in Jacob and disperse them in Israel. He means that Simon will get his share of the land of Canaan and that Levi will be dispersed all over Israel and thereby have no share of the land of Canaan.

We find that Jacob's prophecy has come true.

He then turns to Judah and tells him the future. However, when Judah hears Jacob's harsh words rebuking his three older brothers, he draws back a little. This is why Jacob addresses him directly, whereas he did not do so with Simon and Levi, and says,

"Judah, your brothers will thank you and acknowledge you, your hand will be on your enemy's nape, and your brothers will bow before you.

"Judah, you are like a lion cub. You have elevated yourself by saving my son from being devoured, crouched like a lion—and like a lion, who dares rouse him?

"The scepter shall not depart from Judah, or judges from his offspring, until Shiloh comes, and he will assemble the nations of the earth. One will tie his donkey to a vine and his mule to a vine branch; he will launder his garments in wine and his robe in the blood of the grapes, red eyed from wine and white toothed from milk" (Genesis 49:8–12).

Jacob finds Judah to be the leader among his children. He tells Judah that his brothers will acknowledge him and thank him, because he showed leadership and took responsibility for Benjamin's safety on their second trip to Egypt. Indeed, his brothers were thankful that Judah assumed that responsibility and challenged Joseph, whom he thought was the king of Egypt because he was going to hold Benjamin as his slave.

Jacob's second statement prophesies the future, in which Judah's descendant, specifically King David, will have his hand over his enemy's nape. Indeed, King David expands the land of Israel to its largest boundaries of all time.

Jacob also tells Judah that he will rule over his brothers, and they will bow to him. Here Jacob specifically tells Judah that his offspring will be kings of Israel.

The reason for this good prophecy becomes clear in Jacob's next statement; it is because Judah saved Joseph's life when Simon and Levi conspired to kill him. He tells him that once he makes his mind up, no one will dare deter him from his purpose. Indeed, we see that when King David is just a young boy, he challenges Goliath, the best warrior of the Philistines, even though his brothers tell him it will be suicide. Jacob's prophecy is fulfilled completely, with the exception of the part about Shiloh. Jacob uses the word *Shiloh* to speak of the one who will assemble the nations of the world. It appears that this man will come from the descendants of his son Shelah, the only remaining son of his three original children.

Note that even though Perez and Zerah, who were born of Tamar, are Judah's physical children, he does not consider them his children because Tamar deceived him into making them without his will or understanding. Therefore, in this specific prophecy by Jacob, we learn that the man capable of assembling the nations of the earth will come from his third original son, Shelah.

We further learn that Jacob has coded the essence of this man in the word *Shiloh*, (ש י ל ה). The word *Shiloh* is made of four Hebrew letters: *shin, yod, lamed,* and *hah*. In the order that Jacob relates his prophecy to Judah, it is just a name of a person; however, if one looks at the word carefully and arranges the letters as *shin, lamed,* and then *yod, hah,* or של- יה, one can see that it says, "of God," meaning that this person will be from God, or what we call the Messiah.

Furthermore, these four letters make twenty-four different combinations, only one of which has any meaning associated with God, and that is *shin, lamed, yod,* and *hah,* meaning "of God."

Indeed, it would take a person appointed by God to assemble the nations of the earth. What Jacob says to Judah is that until that person "of God" comes, Judah's descendants will rule Israel. At that time, according to Jacob, there will be such an abundance of wine and milk that people can tie their donkeys and mules to simple vine branches because of their thickness, similar to a tree.

The usage of wine and milk is an indication of plenty, which are the days of the Messiah.

We find that Jacob's prophecy has come true with the exception of the arrival of the person "of God" who will assemble all the nations of the Earth and the state of abundance.

When Jacob prophesies the future for Zebulon, he says to him,

"Zebulon shall settle by the seashore, and he will border Sidon" (Genesis 49:13).

The only thing we learn here is where Zebulon will settle and that ships will anchor in his territory.

Let us study the map of the twelve tribes of Israel as divided by Moses. It appears that the land of Zebulon and Asher were exchanged. Furthermore, so far Jacob has addressed each of his children in the order of their birth; however, here he skips over Issachar and addresses Zebulon.

Why does Jacob skip over Issachar? And why is the land of Zebulon exchanged with the land of Asher?

There are various commentaries suggesting various explanations for Jacob's decision to skip over Issachar. He must have noticed that Issachar is lazy and willing to accept being a laborer and work for someone else rather than making the effort to be his own master, whereas Zebulon works hard to be his own master.

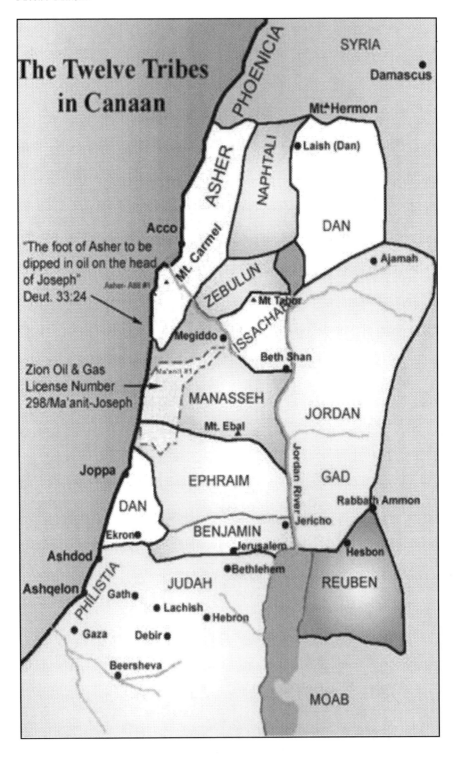

The Twelve Tribes in Canaan

Jacob continues to prophesy the future of Issachar.

He tells him that similar to a strong-boned donkey, he will be resting between the boundaries, and that when he sees tranquility, it will be good. He is willing to accept the role of a laborer rather than being a master of his own (Genesis 49:14–15). Indeed, the land of Issachar is the most fertile land in Israel.

As for Dan, Jacob says,

"Dan will avenge his people, and will judge his people like one of the tribes of Israel. Dan will be a serpent on the highway, a viper by the path that bites the heels of horses so that their riders fall back. For your salvation, O Lord, do I long" (Genesis 49:16–19).

Jacob prophesies that out of the tribe of Dan will come an avenger, and that he will unite all the tribes of Israel as one. Here he is talking about Samson, who in his days united the tribes of Israel as one, and he describes the killing he did with the Philistines with the jaw of an ass. He also sees that Samson will be blinded and tortured and asks for the salvation of the Lord. Indeed, this prophecy of Jacob's comes true, as does his request for Samson's salvation. Note that Samson is blinded because of the fact that he is seduced by Delilah, or Lilith, meaning he has joined the dark forces. That is why his eyesight is taken away and not his life. Since he joins darkness, he has no need to see the light of God. Once he sees God's light within his mind, mainly in response to Jacob's request, he is granted his strength back and all he wishes is to destroy Dagan (or Satan), together with as many Philistines as he can kill (Judges 16:28).

Jacob then prophesies the future of Gad.

He says to him,

"Gad will recruit a regiment and be able to return on its heels" (Genesis 49:19).

What Jacob means here is that the tribe of Gad will assist in conquering the land of Canaan, even though their land is east of the

Jordan River, and that they will return to their land after assisting in the conquering of Canaan, in the same way that they came. Indeed, Gad fights valiantly with the Canaanites until all of Israel is conquered. Oral tradition tells us that he returns to his land without losing one of his troops.

When Jacob comes to Asher, he says to him that Asher will have richness in his bread, and that he will provide royal delicacies (Genesis 49:20).

Jacob's prophecy would have been absolutely correct if Asher and Zebulon had exchanged the land that they were given by Moses. Today's valley of Zebulon has rich soil that can yield all kinds of delicacies, including rich bread.

To Naphtali, Jacob says that he is like a deer in the forest that delivers beautiful sayings (Genesis 49:21). What Jacob means here is that the people of Naphtali are quick on their feet and can cover a great distance quickly with their feet. Indeed, the territory of Naphtali allowed quick movements by feet where other areas of other tribes required horses or donkeys to cover a great distance.

When he came to Joseph, he said to him, "A handsome son is Joseph, a handsome son to the eyes of girls who climbed the walls to gaze upon him. They embittered him and became antagonists; the arrow-tongued men hated him. But his bow was firmly emplaced and his arms were gilded, from the hands of the knight of Jacob, from there the shepherd stone of Israel, from the God of your father who will help you. Shaddai who will bless you, blessing of heaven from above, and blessing of the deep crouching from below, blessing of the bosom and womb. The blessing of your father surpassed the blessing of my parents to the endless bounds of the world's hills; let them be upon Joseph's head and upon the crown of his head like a pure monk to his brothers" (Genesis 49:22–26).

This is indeed a magnificent blessing. Jacob starts the prophecy of Joseph by acknowledging that he is a very handsome man, to the point where the girls of Egypt would climb the city walls to gaze upon him. Then he turns to the act of Joseph being sold to Egypt because of the hatred of his brothers. Jacob refers to Simon and Levi as "they with arrows," meaning that their tongues were like arrows. He notes that they hated Joseph; here, as before, Jacob tells us that he was aware of the hatred of his other sons toward Joseph.

However, Jacob continues and says that Joseph's bow dispersed all the arrows that were sent toward him. Indeed, as we have seen in the story of Joseph, none of the actions caused him mortal death. Then Jacob mentions the shepherd stone of Israel. Here he is talking about the stone that he placed his head upon during the night vision in Beth El. As mentioned earlier, that is the same location where the Temple of Solomon stood many centuries later. What Jacob is saying is that El-Shaddai, who is the shepherd of Israel, and the stone that became the stone of Israel, will bless Joseph, and then he continues with the rest of the blessing, which is very clear.

Jacob's last statement emphasizes his purity like a monk of God among the rest of his brothers. He also mentions to him the blessing of his mother, Rachel, who loved him more than life itself.

To Benjamin, he says, "Benjamin is a predatory wolf: in the morning he will devour his prey, and in the evening he will divide the spoils" (Genesis 49:27).

It is clear that Jacob prophesies that the tribe of Benjamin will be that of great warriors. Indeed, King Saul, who was from the tribe of Benjamin, the first king of Israel, defeated the Philistines, Edom, and Moab.

As Jacob finishes telling his children their future, he orders them to bury him in the same cave where Abraham and Isaac were buried, and the same cave where he buried Leah (Genesis 49:29–31).

After these events, Jacob dies and Joseph orders his physicians to embalm his father. They obey his command (Genesis 50:2). After forty days of his being embalmed, the children of Jacob and all Egypt mourn him for seventy days (Genesis 50:3). Again, we find the number seventy and its significance, as discussed earlier.

Joseph then asks Pharaoh to allow him to travel back to Canaan to bury his father so that he can fulfill the promise he made him (Genesis 50:4–5).

Indeed, Pharaoh gives his permission to Joseph, and Joseph travels to Canaan along with his household, his staff, many of the elders of Egypt, and his brothers, accompanied by many soldiers. So large is the camp that the people of Canaan know it is a very heavy loss to Egypt when they arrive near the Jordan River to mourn Jacob for seven days, in Genesis 50:6–11.

Jacob's children bury him in the cave of Machpelah as he instructed them, and all of them return to Egypt to the land of Goshen (Genesis 50:12–14).

Now that Jacob is dead and buried, Joseph's brothers are afraid he will take revenge upon them; therefore, they approach him and tell him that his father, meaning Jacob, ordered them to tell Joseph to forgive them for the crime they committed against him (Genesis 50:15–17).

As they are speaking to him, Joseph is crying. He tells them not to be afraid, and that he will take care of them and all of theirs. Furthermore, he comforts them and calms them, and Joseph and his brothers settle in Egypt (Genesis 50:17–22).

Joseph lives to be 110 years old and sees his grandchildren and great-grandchildren. When his time to die approaches, he orders his brothers to carry his bones out of Egypt and bury him in the land of his father. He tells them the time will come when they leave Egypt, and makes them swear they will take his bones with them (Genesis 50:23–25).

When Joseph dies, he is embalmed, and they put him in a coffin in Egypt (Genesis 50:26).

Note that when the people of Israel leave Egypt with Moses, they carry with them Joseph's bones and coffin, and later bury him in Shechem (Exodus 3:19).

Conclusion

The book of Genesis is full of wonders.

It is the story of creation and of humanity, and within it, the specific story of the Hebrews.

The biblical story of creation is a very close approximation of the scientific theories of today's most advanced physics.

The Genesis story is so detailed and so accurate in its perception of the universe and its ten dimensions that one is left in awe over the ancient knowledge that existed at that time.

Genesis points to the possibility that there are advanced beings or angels who interacted with selected humans on Earth. This interaction may continue to the present day.

There is no doubt that these beings had access to an immense amount of knowledge and of advanced technology, such as terraforming of planets, teleportation, invisibility or cloaking both people and entire objects, cell regeneration, cloning, and the ability to convert energy into structured matter, among others.

There is also significant probability that the Garden of Eden is indeed a real place on Earth.

We may not find out the original purpose of creating man and woman, since it was diverted by one of these advanced beings and he was punished for it. However, once we were made, they were responsible for our existence and our progress, and took actions to destroy specific people if they deviated from their original intent to the extreme, such as the people of Sodom.

The term *Elohim* definitely refers to angels or advanced beings, while a higher level of the divine also exists. However, these higher levels of the divine are beyond our understanding or knowledge. Only a few selected humans were privileged to have any contact with them.

It seems that these angelic beings can transform themselves into flesh and blood at will, or have the appearance of a flesh and blood being like a man. We see evidence of this transformation several times in Genesis.

The selection of the Hebrews—and specifically Abraham and his seed—as the people who will receive God's laws and, in doing so, enlighten the rest of humanity, is specific. We can see evidence of this throughout the Islamic and Christian nations of the world.

It appears that at least two and a half billion people abide by the laws of Yahweh, the Hebrew God given to Moses in the form of the Ten Commandments.

References

BiblePlaces.com. http://bibleplaces.com/.

Clark, Josh. "Do Parallel Universes Really Exist?," HowStuffWorks, Inc., www.howstuffworks.com/.

Choi doi, Charles Q. (2010). "Molecular Computer Mimics Human Brain," Nature Physics 6:325–326.

Greene, Brian (1998). "A Universe of at Least 10 Dimensions," Columbia University Record, 23:18 (March 27, 1998).

Integrated Environmental Management, Inc. (IEM). www.iem-inc.com.

Kaplan, Rabbi Aryeh 1991. Sefer Yetzirah: The book of creation. York Beach, Maine. Samuel Weiser, Inc.

National Institutes of Health (2009). "Stem Cell Information," US Department of Health and Human Services. http://stemcells.nih.gov/info/scireport/chapter9.asp.

Occult-advances.org. http://occult-advances.org.

Office of Management and Budget, Davis, Eric, W. OMB No. 0704-0188, November 25, 2003, http://www.fas.org/sgp/eprint/teleport.pdf.

Wikipedia, various articles. www.wikipedia.org.

About the Author

Moshe Mazin was born in Baghdad, Iraq. He immigrated to Israel as a small child in 1951 in Operation Ezra and Nehemiah, organized by the state of Israel.

Mr. Mazin is a direct descendant of the original tribes of Joseph and Levi. His ancestors are the ones who were exiled from Jerusalem by King Nebuchadnezzar of Babylon in 586 BC.

Raised in Israel, Mr. Mazin attended the Technion–Israel Institute of Technology, where he studied electrical engineering. He later married an American Jewish woman, had two sons, and settled in the United States. He resides on the north shore of Boston.

Mr. Mazin holds a bachelor of science degree in electrical engineering from the University of Delaware, a master of science degree in electrical engineering from the University of Pennsylvania, and a master's in business administration from Rensselaer Polytechnic Institute in Troy, New York.

Moshe Mazin has forty-eight patents in microelectronic technology.

Printed in the United States
By Bookmasters